Venom

by Marilyn Singer

M Millbrook Press • Minneapolis

To Jean Lerner and her fabulous family,
Liz, Ruth, Dima, and Olympia.
—Marilyn

Millbrook Press
A division of Lerner Publishing Group, Inc.
241 First Avenue North
Minneapolis, MN 55401 USA

For reading levels and more information, look up this title at www.lernerbooks.com.

Library of Congress Cataloging-in-Publication Data

Singer, Marilyn.
    Venom / by Marilyn Singer.
        pages   cm
    Includes bibliographical references (p.) and index.
    ISBN 978-1-58196-043-3
    ISBN 978-1-4677-5179-7 (EB pdf)
    Summary: Learn about venom and the animals that produce
it and use it to survive, including spiders, insects, snakes and
other reptiles, frogs and toads, fish, and ocean invertebrates.
    1. Poisonous arthropoda—Juvenile literature. 2. Poisonous animals—Juvenile literature. 3. Venom—Juvenile literature.
[1. Poisonous arthropoda. 2. Poisonous animals. 3. Venom.] I. Title.
QL434.45 .S56 2007
592.16/5–dc22   OCLC: 79627148

Manufactured in the United States of America
5 – CG – 11/1/14

Venom

Introduction:

Don't Eat, Don't Touch, Don't... Well, Just *Don't!*

All over the world there are animals that can hurt or kill you with a bite, a stab, a sting, or a spit—and others that can hurt or kill if you bite *them*. These creatures can be found in many habitats. They ride the waves. They hide in the sand. They coil around branches. They buzz around the garden. They even sleep in your closet. And every one of them is toxic.

Some animals are *poisonous*. They can make you sick if you eat them or if you absorb their toxins through your skin. They use their poison purely as self-defense against predators, and that includes people. Sometimes a poisonous critter tastes bad enough to make a predator spit it right out. If your dog—or you—were to bite a toxic toad, yuck! But sample some puffer fish, and chances are you wouldn't even know you could be consuming a poison that might kill you.

The most famed toxic critters are *venomous*. This means they must inject their poison—their *venom*—into a victim by means of fangs, teeth, spines, stingers, or spurs. These creatures include snakes, spiders, jellyfish, bees, wasps, scorpions, and a bunch of less familiar animals. But believe it or not, if they can avoid it, none of these creatures wants to waste their venom on inedible YOU!

American toad   or   bullfrog

chuckwalla   or   red-spotted newt

ladybug   or   cricket

sailfish   or   puffer fish

hooded pitohui   or   ring-necked pheasant

Answer: The poisonous ones are the American toad, red-spotted newt, ladybug, puffer fish, and hooded pitohui.

If Looks Could Kill, They Wouldn't Need Poison!

One reason animals use venom is to catch prey—insects, rodents, fish, small mammals, and even others of their own kind. People are too big to be food for venomous animals. However, if by accident or on purpose we harm these creatures, they will strike back to protect themselves. Self-defense is a second major reason animals use venom. A third reason is defense of their family or community.

How dangerous a poisonous or venomous animal is to humans depends on how strong its toxins are, how much of them get into you, and how your body reacts to them.

Choose Your Weapon!

platypus

lion's mane jellyfish

Match the animal with its means of injecting venom.

single stinger
(choose 2)

black widow spider

lionfish

fangs
(choose 2)

spines

scorpion

spurs

rattlesnake

multiple stingers

honeybee

Answer: **single stinger:** scorpion and honeybee; **fangs:** black widow spider and rattlesnake; **spines:** lionfish; **spurs:** platypus; **multiple stingers:** lion's mane jellyfish

Talking about TOXINS

So what exactly are these toxins? Biotoxins are substances that are created by living cells or organisms to harm or kill prey or enemies. They are mostly made up of *proteins*. Proteins carry out important functions in animals' bodies. They form hair, muscles, hemoglobin (part of red blood cells), and *enzymes* (large molecules that speed up chemical reactions). They can make *hormones*, substances that give instructions to various body parts. They can produce *antibodies* to fight infection.

But proteins can also be destroyers. The proteins in various toxins—often in the form of enzymes—attack cells and tissues, disrupt communication between nerve endings, and cause other damage.

Different poisonous or venomous animals produce specific types of toxins or a combination of several kinds. *Neurotoxins* affect the nervous system and brain, making the victim unable to move and breathe. *Hemotoxins* target and destroy red blood cells. *Necrotoxins* destroy all types of tissues. There are other toxins, as well, that specifically affect the heart, the muscles, the kidneys, and other vital organs.

Most venom circulates through the *lymphatic system*. Lymph is a fluid that protects the body from germs. It moves slowly, but thoroughly, and it eventually flows into the bloodstream. Besides little blood vessels called capillaries, there are lymph channels in our skin, and many toxins enter those channels first, although some kinds of venom can go right into the bloodstream. Snake venom, for example, is usually circulated by the lymphatic system, but it can sometimes enter the bloodstream directly—it depends on the size of the molecules of the toxins, the length of the snake's fangs, where on the victim the fangs strike, and other factors.

Some venoms can cause serious injury or even death by triggering a *systemic* (whole body) *reaction*. Other venoms cause a *localized reaction*. For example, bee and wasp ven-

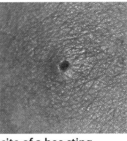
site of a bee sting

oms usually raise a painful lump at the location of the sting—unless the victim is allergic to these toxins. Then he or she may have a systemic reaction.

A rattlesnake's venom *(left)* is mainly hemotoxic, while a cobra's *(right)* is neurotoxic.

When people get stung or bitten by venomous animals, it is called an *envenomation*. Doctors will sometimes treat the victim with *antivenins* to fight the toxins. To make an antivenin, scientists extract venom from the animal, often by getting it to bite cloth stretched across a bottle or tube. Then the venom is purified, dried, and frozen. A weak solution of it is injected into a donor mammal, which is most often a horse or a sheep. The mammal doesn't die. It produces *antibodies*—cells to fight the poison. Blood is drawn from the donor, and the antibodies are extracted and then processed into the antivenin.

Each venom requires a different anti-venin. For some dangerous venoms, there are no known antivenins. Fortunately, most venom is not deadly—at least, not to humans. Other creatures that meet up with venomous animals are not so lucky. As for the venomous critters themselves, most are *immune* to their own toxins—they can't be hurt by them.

Now let's travel the globe to meet some of these killer critters and find out how they use toxins and why. Where shall we start? How about your own house?

"milking" a snake for its venom

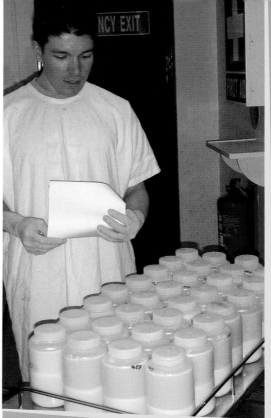

processing antivenin

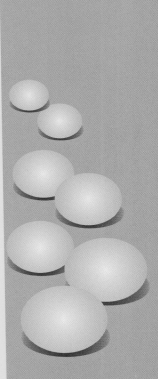

Eggs to the Rescue!

Some people are allergic to horses and can have a bad reaction to antivenin made from their antibodies. In addition, antivenin is expensive to produce and requires drawing a lot of mammal blood, which causes discomfort to the donors. So scientists are working on other ways to produce antivenins.

In India, where snakes bite about three hundred thousand people every year and ten percent of the victims die, biochemists are working on a unique method of making antivenin. They give young hens small doses of snake venom and, as they grow older, the chickens develop special proteins in their blood that act as antidotes against the toxins. These proteins are passed on to their eggs and build up in the yolks. The eggs are then collected, and the proteins are extracted to make the antivenin.

This method could turn out to be safer and a lot less expensive than extracting antivenin from horses. Fifty eggs produce the same amount of antivenin as two pints of horse blood. Since a single hen can lay more than two hundred forty eggs each year—and there are many more hens available than horses—that would produce a lot of antivenin. And that would be good news for people (and for horses, too).

Home Is Where the *Venom* Is

You are not the only animal that thinks your home is cozy. Many uninvited critters live with us. Some—such as mice, rats, houseflies, bedbugs, fleas, and lice—aren't toxic. Others are. For one familiar group of these venomous creatures, our homes provide not only food and dark corners to hide in, but also perfect places to spin webs. What are they? You guessed it: spiders.

Eensy-Weensy Spiders (and Their Bigger Cousins)

Spiders are not insects. They are *arachnids*. Insects have six legs, and their bodies have three sections (head, thorax, and abdomen). Arachnids have eight legs, mouth parts, and their bodies consist of two parts, the *cephalothorax* and the *abdomen*. There are close to forty thousand species of spiders, as compared to about a million species of insects.

Most spiders are meat-eaters, and almost all are venomous. They produce venom in special glands and inject it through the fangs at the tips of their *chelicerae*—their mouthparts. The shape of their fangs, straight or curved, differs among species. Their venom paralyzes or kills prey. The idea that it also helps turn the prey into liquid food is probably untrue. Spiders do liquefy prey, but they use digestive juices from their gut that they throw up, several times if necessary, onto the prey.

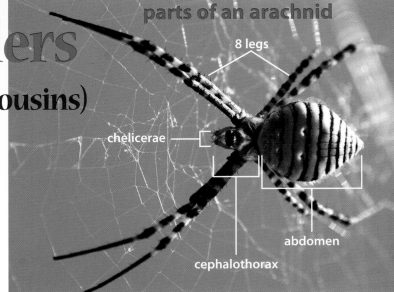

parts of an arachnid
8 legs
chelicerae
abdomen
cephalothorax

Once the victim is liquefied, the spider can then suck it up through its specialized mouth, which is a slit and has hairs that act as a filter.

Smaller spiders eat insects and other spiders. If the prey is small enough, they may not even bother with venom. They will just crush or chew it with their chelicerae and liquefy it with their digestive juices. Larger spiders eat insects and other spiders, too, but they may also feed on mice, birds, frogs, lizards, and snakes—sometimes even poisonous ones.

Different types of spiders hunt in different ways. Some spin sticky silken webs to catch prey or make "trigger" lines over burrows that alert the spider to prey walking over them. Some cast silken nets. Others don't use silk for hunting at all—they stalk prey on the ground.

Many spiders use silk to wrap up their victims. This prevents the prey from struggling and hurting the spider. It also means the prey can be stored and eaten later. Some spiders bite first, then wrap their prey; others wrap first, then bite.

And they're just waiting to bite you, right? Nope. Few spiders can or want to harm you. Like other venomous animals, arachnids use a lot of their body's resources to produce venom. So, they won't waste it unless it's absolutely necessary. Furthermore, most have fangs that are too small to penetrate our skin or venom that is too weak to hurt us. The **common house spider** (*Achaearanea*

spider and egg sac

tepidariorum), for example, is harmless to people. In fact, like many of its cousins, it's actually helpful because it rids our homes of a variety of insect pests, including houseflies and mosquitoes.

Spiders that *can* bite people usually do so only if they are grabbed or otherwise trapped against our skin, or if they need to protect their egg sacs or young. Most prefer to run away. Even when their fangs do pierce our skin, spiders often "dry" bite—they don't expel venom.

Many people think they've been bitten by spiders when they've actually been zapped by something else. Spiders tend to bite just once. A row or group of bites usually means fleas, bed bugs, mites, or mosquitoes are what got you.

Tarantulas!!! *Hairy?* Yes. *Deadly?* Not Really.

Check out any horror film featuring spiders, and you're likely to see large, hairy **tarantulas** with deadly fangs, often crawling on the victim's bed. But don't believe everything you see in the movies. Although it's true that these creatures of deserts, rainforests, and other habitats do sometimes enter homes, they are rarely lethal. The bites of North and South American tarantulas are generally no worse than bee stings—and they usually don't bite at all (although they have some relatives that are more dangerous). They don't even mind being handled, which is why some people keep them as pets. If you ever get to hold a tarantula, be careful never to drop it. Its abdomen is fragile, and the spider can be badly injured in a fall.

Tarantulas have a second defense besides venom: They kick off microscopic *urticating*—irritating—hairs, usually from the topside of their abdomen, to blind and otherwise deter enemies. The hairs can sting and itch human eyes, noses, and skin, but they contain no venom at all. Tarantulas that are used to being handled are less likely to flick these hairs.

A Few Spiders Miss Muffet Should Avoid

So, which spiders *are* the big biters? In the U.S., most painful spider bites come from the **yellow sac spider** (*Cheiracanthium inclusum*), the **red-backed jumping spider** (*Phidippus johnsoni*), and a few other species found around our homes. A jumping spider's bite may cause localized swelling and pain. A sac spider's bite can be quite painful, and the wound may take a long time to heal. Its venom can also cause headache, fever, nausea, dizziness, and even shock. But serious problems from these spider bites are rare.

Only three types of spiders are considered truly dangerous to people in this country: the **black widow** (*Latrodectus mactans*) and other widow species, the **brown recluse** (*Loxosceles reclusa*) and some of its relatives, and the **hobo spider** (*Tegenaria agrestis*).

hobo spider

Shiny black with a red hourglass mark on its belly, the black widow is the best known and most venomous spider in America. It likes dark places, including basements, sheds, woodpiles, and outdoor toilets, where it spins a tangled, criss-cross web. Only the females bite. But do they live up to their name? Do they really kill and eat their mates? Yes, occasionally, they do—in order to get enough nourishment to lay eggs. However, when it comes to harming people, these ladies are rather shy and tend to run away rather than attack.

yellow sac spider

red-backed jumping spider

black widow spider

Black widows, found all over the U.S., rarely kill humans, but they can make us quite sick, causing not only fever, nausea, and pain, but also high blood pressure and severely rigid muscles. In the worst cases, a victim can have trouble breathing. A black widow's neurotoxic venom is fifteen times more potent than a rattlesnake's! But it's not as dangerous to people because a spider injects much less venom than a snake does.

There are widow species all over the world, and one of them, the **brown widow** (*Latrodectus geometricus*), which has a yellow hourglass mark, has now moved into the Mississippi Gulf Coast region. It probably made its way there from Florida, hitching a ride with imported plants, food, furniture, or building materials. The brown widow is a very timid spider, preferring to curl up into a ball and drop to the ground as its main defense. When it does bite, it is to protect its egg sac. Fortunately, its venom seems to be far less potent than its cousin's and causes mostly a localized reaction.

My Roommate Is a FROG

Colombian lesser black

Although tarantulas eat frogs (as well as insects, lizards, and small mammals), several species, such as the **Colombian lesser black** (*Xenesthis immanis*), will peacefully share their burrows with these amphibians. Scientists guess that the frogs protect the spiders' eggs by eating ants that would otherwise feed on those eggs. And the spiders protect the frogs from being eaten by other predators.

brown widow spider

characteristic violin marking of a brown recluse spider

The **brown recluse** lives in the South-Central and the Midwest states. It is found in areas such as in closets, behind furniture, and on the floor. People are most likely to be bitten if they put on clothes or shoes they haven't worn in a while or if they roll on the spider in bed. The recluse's venom is necrotoxic. Its bite may be painless when delivered, but later the area often becomes swollen and tender and develops into a wound that takes weeks or even months to heal.

You can recognize a recluse by the violin-shaped mark on its head and back (the neck of the violin points toward the rear). If you have a magnifying glass, you can also see that, unlike most other spiders, it has six eyes instead of eight.

The **hobo spider** was originally a field dweller from Europe. It hitched a ride on cargo ships bound for northwestern America and quickly adapted to rural areas and small towns with cool, moist climates. Hobo spiders live in grassy areas, amid rubble, and around foundations. The males occasionally enter houses. The effects of its bite are similar to that of the brown recluse.

The hobo spider is a type of funnel-web weaver. Its flat web has a funnel at the back where the spider waits for prey. Unlike the webs of many other spiders, this spider's web isn't sticky. It trips up the prey's legs, and then the spider dashes out to bite the victim.

Hobo spiders are generally not aggressive. But another funnel-web weaver, one more related to the tarantula, is. The **Sydney funnel-web spider** (*Atrax robustus*), which nests in shaded garden areas around Sydney, a large city in Australia, is quicker to attack—particularly the male, which is five or six times more venomous than the female. Like a miniature horror movie monster, the spider rears up and threatens you right back, with potent venom dripping from its fangs.

The worst time to meet this arachnid is when the males are wandering around looking for mates. The male's neurotoxic venom contains a special substance called *robustoxin*. It is not particularly harmful to dogs or cats, but it can be fatal to humans and other primates.

adult and juvenile brown recluse spiders

As the males wander, they may enter a house and hide in clothing or bedding, where they're more likely to encounter people. They also occasionally fall into swimming pools, but they don't immediately drown. They can trap a small air bubble in their abdomen hairs and stay alive (and capable of biting) for hours underwater.

Because of its potent venom and the fact that it lives in a city of four million people, this arachnid is one of the most dangerous spiders in the world. In the past, people have died from its bite. Fortunately, there is now an antivenin available to treat victims.

Sydney funnel-web spider

Blue Mountains funnel-web spider being milked.

That Which Doesn't Kill You Might Just Cure You

Venoms are necessary for the production of antivenins. But that's not all they're good for. Scientists are actively studying spider venoms to discover treatments and cures for a variety of disorders. For example, they have isolated a chemical in tarantula venom that may help stop atrial fibrillation (irregular heartbeat), a major cause of death.

In addition, spider venom may prove to be a farmer's good friend. The **Blue Mountains funnel-web spider** (*Hadronyche versuta*) is a species whose bite is lethal to humans and other beings. Australian biochemists have isolated the neurotoxins in its venom that paralyze insects. In the venom, there are individual substances that target specific prey. Scientists are hoping to design insecticides that will be toxic to bugs, but not to anything else. The Blue Mountains funnel-web spider is not the only species that may be the source of pest control. There are thousands of arachnids yet to be studied—and quite a few scientists willing to study them.

Ticked off

Ticks are also arachnids. They can carry a wide variety of serious diseases, such as Rocky Mountain spotted fever and Lyme disease, which are caused by bacteria and other organisms, not venom. Only one known tick-borne illness is caused by a neurotoxin: tick paralysis. The tick transmits this neurotoxin through its saliva as it feeds, and the arachnid has to be embedded—attached—to the host for a while to do so. The symptoms are weakness, lack of muscle control, and eventual paralysis, which can lead to respiratory failure and death. Fortunately, the illness usually clears up if the tick is removed quickly enough.

To prevent tick bites, veterinarians suggest insecticides for your pets. For people in tick-infested areas, doctors recommend repellents and also protective clothing, such as long pants tucked into your socks.

Although several varieties of ticks carry this neurotoxin, most don't seem to cause the illness. However, in Australia there is a species known as the **paralysis tick** (*Ixodes holocyclus*). Dogs, cats, and people, especially children, have been victims of its potent toxin. But possums and bandicoots have not. These two families of Australian mammals are immune.

Ticks must be attached to a host to transmit diseases or neurotoxins.

The brushtail possum *(top)* and the longnosed bandicoot *(bottom)* are immune to the paralysis tick's venom.

They've Got Legs— and They Know How to Use Them

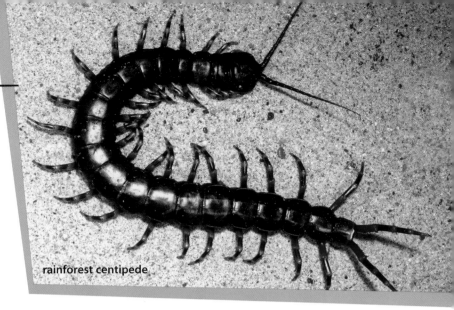
rainforest centipede

In our homes, spiders aren't the only venomous critters that find good pickings among the many insects that live with us. **Centipedes** (*Scutigera*) like to make a meal out of common household bugs, too. In the wild, they like moist forest floors. In our homes, they've adapted to the dampness of our bathrooms and basements.

Centipedes are not insects. They have many body segments and fifteen to one hundred and fifty pairs of legs to go with them. The first is a pair of claws called *prehensors* that have adapted for grasping prey and injecting venom. Some of these critters, such as the colorful twelve-inch-long, bat-eating, **rainforest centipede** (*Scolopendra gigantea*), deliver painful envenomations. The small **house centipede** (*Scutigera coleoptrata*) in your bathtub may also be able to stab, but it can't cause you much injury—and it gets rid of lots of pests, including bed bugs!

Millipedes, relatives of the centipedes, have twenty to one hundred body segments, most with two pairs of legs each. Living outdoors, they eat leaves and decaying vegetation, and most are not venomous at all. They have a tough exoskeleton, and their main defense is to roll into a tight, hard ball.

But some species are poisonous, such as the **yellow-spotted millipede** (*Harpaphe haydeniana*).

Like a few uncommon centipede species, they emit acid or liquid hydrogen cyanide—a toxin sometimes featured in murder mysteries—to repel predators, such as ants and toads. Although millipedes don't discharge enough of these poisons to hurt people, it's a good idea not to touch your eyes after handling this species.

Black lemurs, primates found in Madagascar, and South American capuchin monkeys are known to rub millipedes on themselves, using the poison to repel insect pests.

house centipede

Spiders, centipedes, and millipedes are helpful animals with every right to live. But when it comes to sharing our house and yard with these beings, most of us would probably prefer roommates that don't stab, bite, or ooze.

millipede

yellow-spotted millipede

Mary, Mary, Quite Contrary, How Does Your Garden Sting?

What is lovelier than a garden? Roses and daisies—they're a feast for the eyes and nose. Tomatoes and peppers—they're a treat for the taste buds. Yes, a garden is a delight for you, and also for things that sting.

honeybee

Bee Careful

Zipping past your petunias is one of the most dangerous animals in America—one you might see every summer day. It kills more people in the U.S. than any other venomous animal. Yet most of us are happy to see it fly by, because without it we might not have such lovely petunias at all. What is this bold critter? None other than the **honeybee** (*Apis mellifera*).

There are different types of bees. Many spread pollen to help our gardens grow. Some, such as **carpenter bees** (*Xylocopa*), are solitary. They nest in burrows or holes that the females carve in dead wood. The bees we are most familiar with—**bumblebees** (*Bombus terrestris*) and honeybees—live communally.

Each colony has a strict social structure. The queen produces eggs. The female workers take care of the hive. They perform tasks such as gathering pollen and nectar, making honey, fighting off intruders, and building and repairing cells out of wax to store food and house the *larvae*—the young. The males, called *drones*, don't work at all. Nor can they sting. They mate in midair with the queen and die shortly afterwards.

Almost all bees are vegetarians, living on nectar and pollen from flowers. They use their venom strictly to protect themselves or their colonies. Oddly enough, some **stingless bees** (*Meliponini*), which have no venom at all, are the only meat-eaters in this family. They live on *carrion* (rotting flesh) and other animal material instead of pollen and are nicknamed the "vulture bees."

The bee's stinger has developed over time from what was once its *ovipositor*— its egg-laying tube. In all but one species, the honeybee's

stingless "vulture bee"

stinger is barbed to hook and remain in the victim and to keep pumping venom. As the bee flies away, the insect's abdomen tears, and the bee soon dies. Sometimes its victim dies, too—especially if many bees have stung it.

When workers near their hive sense danger, the bees give off an *alarm pheromone*—a chemical signal they can detect. This alerts all the hive's inhabitants, and they become ready to attack if necessary. If any of them *do* strike, the glands responsible for producing the alarm pheromone detach along with the stinger and keep giving off the signal to attack.

Bee stings are painful for a reason. American entomologist Justin O. Schmidt feels that pain is responsible for the insect's survival. The pain of the sting fools a predator into thinking that the bee has caused more serious damage than it actually has, and thus the victim will avoid it in future.

It's certainly true that although it hurts a lot, the venom from a single sting is not strong enough to kill most animals, including humans—unless you are allergic to the venom. Some sources say that as many as four people in one thousand have systemic reactions to bee stings. When allergic people are stung, they can go into *anaphylactic shock*—their whole bodies react so badly that they may stop breathing. To survive, they need an *epinephrine* shot, followed by a trip to the doctor or emergency room. There are kits with epinephrine syringes available for people with this allergy. The high number of allergic people, plus the fact that bees and humans are common neighbors, explains why these insects are dangerous.

queen bee

Bee Healthy: Apitherapy

Apitherapy is the use of natural products from bees—including pollen, honey, and venom—to cure a wide range of disorders. Bee venom has at least forty different ingredients. The main one is *mellitin*, which is responsible for the "ouch" in a bee sting. It is also a powerful anti-inflammatory agent. For centuries, apitherapists have treated arthritis and other inflammations of the joints by allowing bees to sting patients on certain points of their bodies.

Today, live bees are still used, but some practitioners prefer venom-filled syringes instead. There have been few documented scientific studies, but many patients claim that the venom helps them.

Currently, mellitin is being investigated as a treatment for multiple sclerosis and for cancer, among other diseases.

Bees for Breakfast

bee-eater

What kind of crazy bird eats bees? A **bee-eater**, of course (example: *Merops nubicoides*). These brightly colored residents, found in Africa, Asia, Australia, and southern Europe, pursue many kinds of flying insects, but honeybees are their favorites. They catch the bees, take them to a perch, and remove their stingers by pounding and rubbing the insects against a hard surface.

A bee-eater isn't interested in a sitting bee or other bug, even if that insect lands right next to it. These birds will only hunt things on the wing.

Will the Real Killer Bees Please Stand... er... Fly Up?

Which of these is the *real* KILLER BEE?

1 — European honeybee

2 — Africanized honeybee

3 — bumblebee

4 — cicada killer

Answer: Number 2—and yes, it looks just like its relative, Number 1.

Buzzin' Cousins

Honeybees were originally brought to the Americas from Europe in the early seventeenth century. Then, in 1956, some colonies of African honeybees were imported to South America to improve the bee industry in Brazil. This African variety produced a lot of honey, and the bees seemed better suited to the warmer climate than their European relatives. The following year, some of the bees escaped from an experimental *apiary* (the place where beehives are kept), and they began to interbreed with the European bees already living there. The **Africanized honeybees,** or **killer bees**, were their offspring. They are now found in Central America and parts of the U.S., as well as South America.

The reason they are called killer bees is not because their venom is any more dangerous than that of the European bees. It isn't. They got their name because they defend their colonies more aggressively. For example, they may attack a person for approaching too near a hive—something European bees are less likely to do. When they do attack, killer bees sting in greater numbers and for a longer time, and they will pursue their enemies farther from their nest. A person who isn't allergic to bee venom can, perhaps, survive as many as three hundred stings. A swarm of killer bees has been known to deliver *ten thousand* stings.

Are you likely to be pursued by an American colony of killer bees? Not really. But let's suppose a swarm comes after you. What should you do? You should *not* jump into water—the bees will be waiting for you when you get out. Instead, get inside a car or building, or just run! Killer bees may be fierce and persistent, but they're also slow, and, even though they fly further from their hive than European bees, they still don't want to travel too far. There's a good chance that you can outrace them—though you may have to run several hundred yards before they give up.

Wasp-Waisted

Wasps and bees are close relatives. In fact, bees—and ants—evolved from wasps. Usually less hairy than bees, wasps are known for their very narrow "waists" between the thorax and abdomen. They do not make honey or wax, and they have smooth stingers, which means they can sting over and over without dying.

The wasps we most often encounter are the social wasps—creatures that live in groups—such as **hornets** (*Vespa*), **yellow jackets** (*Vespula*), and **paper wasps** (*Polistes*). All of them make different types of papery nests, sometimes in troublesome places, such as on door hinges, inside porch lights, or under tables. Disturb a well-developed nest, and you could get zapped.

Solitary wasps—critters that live alone—can also sting in self-defense, but they mainly use their venom to paralyze spiders or insects. Like bees, these wasps feed largely on nectar—when they are adults. As babies, they need a lot more protein, and that means meat.

The **great golden digger wasp** *(Sphex ichneumoneus)* will sting prey, such as a katydid, and then drag the victim into its burrow nest in the ground. The **tarantula hawk**, aka tarantula wasp (example: *Pepsis formosa*), a desert species, will attack a tarantula many times its size, paralyze the spider, and manage to lug it to the spider's nest, or sometimes the wasp's own burrow. This wasp's sting is especially painful to people, though not lethal.

A **potter wasp** (*Eumenes*) or a **mud dauber wasp** (*Trypoxylon politum*) carries its prey—a spider or insect, depending on the wasp species—into its pot or pipe-shaped clay nest, which is often found on buildings. Then, the wasp lays an egg, generally on the prey. When the egg hatches, the larva eats the meat. The paralyzed, but still-living prey is not only high in protein, but also fresh.

hornet

paper wasp

potter wasp

It Ain't an Ant

It looks like a hairy ant. It crawls on the ground like a hairy ant. But the **velvet ant** (example: *Dasymutilla occidentalis*) is actually a solitary wasp. Males are winged, but females are wingless. In most species, females parasitize other solitary wasps, as well as solitary bees. They enter their victims' nests, open the cells where the larvae are developing, and lay eggs on them so their youngsters can hatch and feed on these insects.

Adult velvet ants drink mostly nectar. They are not aggressive creatures. They try to run from enemies, and they make squeaking sounds when disturbed. In America, the velvet ant's painful venomous sting has earned it the nickname "cow killer," although it really can't kill any cattle.

In Africa, two species of velvet ants parasitize **tsetse flies** (*Glossina*), which carry sleeping sickness, a serious disease that affects horses, cattle, and people. Scientists hope that velvet ants may someday be used as the biological control of these harmful flies.

velvet ant
(female)

tsetse fly

Color Me Toxic

Although there are many species of solid-colored wasps and bees, when we think of these insects, we think of flashy stripes: orange and black or yellow and black. These colors and patterns are *aposematic*—they warn enemies that these critters are venomous. Once a bird, amphibian, or other predator attempts to sample a stinging wasp or bee, it will hesitate to try another. The sacrifice of a few insects ensures the survival of many more.

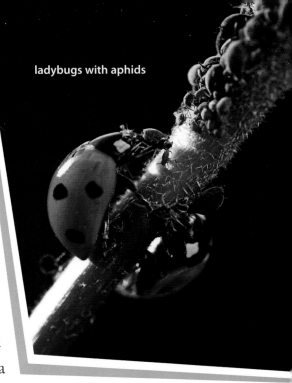
ladybugs with aphids

Aposematism is a useful device. So is *mimicry*—animals imitating other animals. Some nonvenomous creatures imitate venomous ones. Wasps and bees have many stingless mimics. Several of these copycats, such as the **American hover fly** (*Metasyrphus americanus*) and its relatives, use their colors to protect themselves from being eaten by birds and reptiles. Certain **robber flies** (example: *Dasyllis haemorrhoa*) look just like honeybees so they can stalk and eat the bees. But if you examine these mimics, you'll see that, like all flies, they have one pair of wings instead of the two pairs that bees and wasps possess.

Other garden insects' warning colors announce that they are poisonous to eat. The poison is generally not strong enough to kill predators. It makes more sense for the survival of a species to sicken, not slaughter enemies so they'll learn to avoid this prey in the future.

The most familiar of these aposematic insects are two garden favorites: the orange and black **ladybug** (example: *Coccinella septempunctata*), which is a type of beetle, and the **monarch butterfly** (*Danaus plexippus*).

Who doesn't like ladybugs? Aphids—because ladybugs eat them. But neither do many frogs, toads, birds, and lizards. Ladybugs taste terrible! If the beetle's warning coloration isn't enough to deter a hunter, it will reflex-bleed, which means it will ooze yellowish blood from its leg joints. The fluid contains toxins and has a bad odor. A predator will quickly realize by smell, taste, or both that a ladybug is bad eats.

The monarch butterfly feeds on nectar from a variety of flowers. But in its caterpillar stage, it eats only toxic milkweed leaves and, as a result, it too becomes toxic—and remains toxic, right into adulthood. Birds and other beings that taste this butterfly learn from its Halloween colors that they don't want a second bite.

monarch caterpillar

monarch butterfly

monarch butterfly

viceroy butterfly

rattlebox moth

I'm the King!
No, I'm the King!

Monarchs and other toxic butterflies have many mimics. One well-known monarch imitator is the **viceroy butterfly** (*Limenitis archippus*). For years, entomologists—insect scientists—thought that the viceroy was not toxic, that it was just fooling predators into thinking it was. This type of mimicry is called *Batesian mimicry*. But entomologists now believe that viceroys, too, are toxic.

In the tropical Americas, poisonous **passion vine butterflies** (*Heliconius*), which feed on the cyanide-laced nectar and pollen from passion flowers, also have toxic mimics. When a toxic species imitates another toxic species, it's called *Mullerian mimicry*. What's the point of this form of imitation? Birds and other predators have to learn just one pattern. Then they will leave all the toxic animals with that pattern alone.

passion vine butterfly

Pretty Poison

Other butterflies and their close relatives also become poisonous from their diet. Among these are various species of **tiger moths** of the Arctiidae family, many of which are aposematic. If they are touched, some secrete poisonous foam from glands in their thorax.

tiger moth

Spiders and other predators will avoid these insects. It's a good idea for people to avoid touching these foaming flyers, too, as the froth of certain species can burn human skin.

Rattlebox moths (*Utetheisa ornatrix*) are members of the frothing tiger moth clan. The females get a unique wedding present from the males. The female moths are born toxic, but as they reach reproductive age, they need more toxins to protect their many eggs from certain wasps that attack them. During mating, males transmit this extra poison to the females, and the females, in turn, pass it to the eggs.

frothing rattlebox moth

Nasty, Hairy Caterpillars

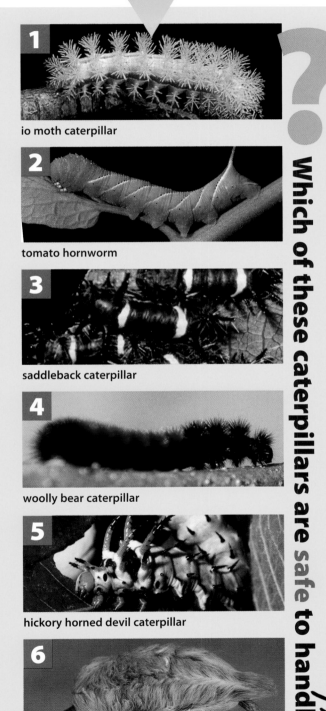

1. io moth caterpillar
2. tomato hornworm
3. saddleback caterpillar
4. woolly bear caterpillar
5. hickory horned devil caterpillar
6. puss moth caterpillar

Which of these caterpillars are safe to handle?

Answers: 2, 4, 5

Insects are popular prey, so they've had to develop many forms of protection in order to survive, and that means quite a few are bound to be toxic. Some, like the monarchs and the tiger moths, are poisonous. Others, such as the **io moth** (*Automeris io*) and **saddleback caterpillars** (*Sibine stimule*), are urticating insects with spines that easily break off. And in their case, the spines contain toxins that pour out to irritate predators, making human skin itch and burn.

The spines of the cute **puss moth caterpillar** (*Megalopyge opercularis*) are covered with a thick coat of reddish-brown hairs. This caterpillar's toxins are the most severe. Besides getting a skin rash, its victims may experience headaches, nausea, weakness, and shock.

Adult moths don't have venomous spines, but the females of some species will gather the spines from their own cast-off caterpillar skins and use them to cover and protect their eggs with a cozy, toxic quilt!

monarch caterpillar

Hands Off These Insects, Too

Blister beetles (example: *Epicauta fabricii*) will eat your flowers or your vegetables, but predators can't eat them. They're poisonous. If you

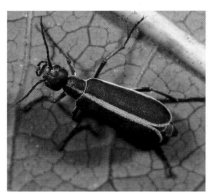
blister beetle

handle them, some species will ooze the toxic substance, *cantharidin*, from their legs. This chemical will raise blisters on your skin, but the same toxin is used in ointments to cure warts!

Some animals, such as hedgehogs, frogs, and a variety of spiders, can tolerate cantharidin. One insect that's known to thrive on it is the **fire-colored beetle**, *Neopyrochroa flabellata*. It eats the chemical to protect itself from predators. A male will secrete some between its eyes and offer this toxic treat to a female. If she accepts his gift,

fire-colored beetle

he'll transmit another load of cantharidin when they mate. Like the rattlebox moth, the female fire-colored beetle then passes on the poison to her eggs.

Some **assassin bugs** can stomach monarch butterflies. Some eat other insects. And a few feast on human blood. As their name suggests, they hunt very quickly. All assassin bugs have a

sharp, curved *rostrum*, or beak, to pierce their prey. Within the rostrum are several fused *stylets*—needle-like tubes that are used to inject

young wheel bug (assassin bug)

venom, which paralyzes and liquefies the victim, and then to suck up the prey. One species, the **wheel bug** (*Arilus cristatus*), has such fast-acting venom that, once bitten, a caterpillar more than four hundred times this predator's weight can die in just ten seconds.

Some assassin bugs can pierce human skin. The wheel bug's bite is said to be the most painful of any insect. But it isn't eager to

bloodsucking conenose

bite you. More dangerous is another species, the **bloodsucking conenose** (*Triatoma sanguisuga*) found in Central and South America, where it enters homes to feed on human blood. It is nicknamed the "kissing bug," because it can painlessly pierce a victim's lips, eyelids, or ears. What makes it dangerous is not its venom, but Chagas disease, that can be transmitted through its feces, which it sometimes deposits on the person it bites. This illness may result in heart and digestive problems and even death.

mosquito

The Most Dangerous
Insect of All

The most dangerous insect—perhaps the most dangerous animal—in the world has no stinger or spines. In fact, it's not venomous or poisonous at all, yet it sickens or kills 700,000,000 people worldwide each year, and countless other animals, as well. What is this scary creature? A female **mosquito** (example: *Anopheles punctipennis*).

There are many species of mosquitoes. All of them develop in water or moisture. The larvae hatch from eggs, grow, pupate, and emerge a week later as adults. Males feed on nectar. Females also feed on nectar, but most need blood to produce eggs, and they don't care where it comes from—a lion, a deer, a robin, a poodle, or *you*.

They find their victims by sensing body heat, sweat, and carbon dioxide, given off when we breathe. They use their sharp, needle-like *proboscis*—tubular mouth—with fused stylets to inject saliva that contains *anticoagulants* (substances to keep the victim's blood from clotting) and to draw up that blood.

Through its saliva, mosquitoes can transmit a host of diseases and parasites, including yellow fever, malaria, West Nile fever, encephalitis, and heartworms. Not all mosquitoes cause disease, but their itchy bites can make our days and nights miserable.

So what are mosquitoes good for? Food! That may not please *you*, but it does please bats, dragonflies, frogs, toads, and many other animals, both toxic and non-toxic, that feast on these whining flies.

Femme Fatale Fireflies

Fireflies are magical signs of summer. They use their famous lights to find mates. The males and females of each species use specific patterns to "talk" to each other. Fireflies are also poisonous. Or rather the *Photinus* species are. Their rear ends produce not only their light-making chemicals, but also compounds called *lucibufagins*, which are toxic to a whole host of animals, including spiders, lizards, and toads.

Now here's where it gets weird. Female fireflies of the *Photuris* species can't produce their own lucibufagins. So how do they get them? They pretend to be *Photinus* babes, flashing their signal at *Photinus* males. When a male takes the bait, the female *Photuris* kills and eats him, acquiring his toxins. Then she is protected against predators.

If you thought the black widow spider was a *femme fatale*, she's nothing compared to this gal!

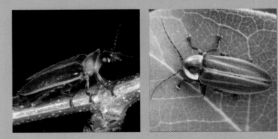

Photinus   *Photuris*

Don't Sit on the Grass!

Grass. It's our favorite natural carpet. We plant it as lawns and meadows for homes, parks, and other areas. It plants itself to create prairies, savannahs, and other grasslands. We're not the only beings who like grass. Some turf lovers are critters we'd just as soon not meet.

A Field Day for Ants

What's a picnic without sandwiches, chips, lemonade, and . . . venom? Who's bringing the toxins? Ants, of course.

Ants are members of the same order as bees and wasps. But while some bees and wasps are solitary, ants, on the other hand, are always social. Their nests are found underground, in trees, and in buildings. Some species live in large, well-ordered colonies that may number in the millions. Colonies may even join together to form supercolonies, covering a wide area of land. Female workers are wingless. Males and young queens have wings, and, among many colonies during mating season, they fly out to establish new nests and colonies. Then the wings drop off or are pulled off.

Ants are found in grasslands, as well as deserts, temperate woodlands, and rainforests. Most of them are harmless, such as the little black ants (*Monomorium minimum*) that invade our picnics and our houses for food. But some species use their rear ends to sting or spray, and nobody wants to picnic around them.

ant colony

Ants That Sting

large fire ant mound

In America, the nastiest of these stingers may well be imported **fire ants** (*Solenopsis invicta* and *Solenopsis richteri*). Fire ants arrived in the U.S. by hitching rides on ships from South America. They build big mound nests, two feet wide and up to three feet high, in fields and lawns. They are especially fond of golf courses. Worker ants exit from tunnels that can extend as much as ten yards from the mound. They are omnivorous and will use their venom to paralyze or kill many kinds of small ground-nesting animals for food.

They also aggressively defend their nests. When an enemy threatens, a fire ant will clamp on with its jaws and spin in a circle, stinging over and over with its rear end. A single fire ant's stings cause itchy, burning blisters, but they're usually not deadly. However, when one ant stings, its alarm pheromone alerts the other ants, which come rushing out of the ground. No animal wants to face a whole colony of two hundred thousand stinging ants!

fire ant

red harvester ant

Some people confuse **red harvester ants** (*Pogonomyrmex barbatus*), the native American species usually sold for ant farms, with fire ants. They can also sting, but they are non-aggressive and non-invasive—they don't take over other species' habitats. In fact, they are being driven out by the imported fire ants in parts of the country. The decline of this species has led, in part, to the decline of its predator, the Texas horned lizard. In addition, the lizard and its eggs are the prey of the fire ants.

Imported fire ants have invaded other countries, too. Australia is currently doing battle with these pests. This continent already has its share of fierce stingers, including the **bulldog** or **jumping ants** (*Myrmecia*), known for their huge jaws and savage grip. Along with the fire ants, the bulldog ants have surely ruined more than one picnic. However, recent studies suggest that their toxins may also hold the key to lowering high blood pressure. So perhaps some picnickers will forgive them.

Fire Ant
Foes

In South America, many species of anteaters and armadillos eat fire ants. In the American Southwest, we have only one type of armadillo to do the job. But even if we had more species, armadillos alone can't conquer these insects. It takes a bug to eliminate a bug.

Female **phorid flies** (*Pseudacteon*) are attracted to fire ants swarming over a disturbed mound. Each fly selects an individual ant and attacks it in flight, injecting an egg into the ant's thorax with its hook-like *ovipositor*. The larva hatches and moves through the ant's body and into its head, killing its host.

Originally from Brazil and Argentina where they keep down the fire ant population, phorid flies are being carefully and experimentally released at various sites in the U.S. So far, they seem to destroy nothing but the ants. Since fire ant mounds are disturbed by armadillos, this combination of a mammal and a fly may prove a powerful force against these stingers—and a blessing to American picnickers and golfers.

bulldog ant

army ant

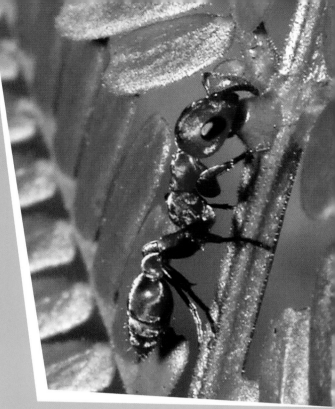
bullhorn acacia ant

An Army of Stingers

Ants are social not only near their nests. Sometimes they travel together to hunt—and no group of marching ants forms a scarier image than the **army ants** (*Eciton burchelli*) of South and Central America. They migrate regularly to find new camping and hunting grounds. For two or three nights, in groups of one hundred thousand to two million, they march, moving in organized patterns, attacking animals in their path. First, they sting their victims, and then they tear them apart with jaws so powerful that native Central American people have used the ants as sutures to hold wounds together until they healed.

Army ants mostly eat insects and spiders—about fifty thousand in a single day—but they have been known to attack mice, rats, snakes, birds, and even large mammals. Their victims often die of shock.

Do these ants devour people? No. No matter what you see in Hollywood movies, people can easily step aside and watch the ants pass—a parade that may take hours. Even when the ants enter houses, the human inhabitants can just take their livestock and leave—and thank the ants for clearing their homes of vermin. The truth is that these insects are threatened by people rather than vice versa, as we claim more and more of their habitat for human use.

Together Wherever We Sting

A symbiotic relationship is one that benefits two species that live together. Sometimes those two species are both animals. But sometimes—as in the case of the **bullhorn acacia** (*Acacia cornigera*) and the **bullhorn acacia ant** (*Pseudomyrmex ferruginea*)—one is a tree and the other is an animal.

Most acacia trees have bitter chemicals in their leaves to protect them from being eaten. Bullhorn acacias don't. What they have instead are ants living in their hollow thorns. The trees provide special food for the ants, and the ants provide defense for the trees, rushing out to sting any creatures that want to feast on the foliage.

bullet ant

The Mother of All Stings

Jason O. Schmidt has been stung by almost every bee, wasp, and ant in the world, so he created the "Schmidt Sting Pain Index" to describe the type and severity of the pain from different kinds of stings. According to Schmidt, the bullhorn acacia ant's sting is worse than the fire ant's, the red harvester's is more painful than the acacia ant's, and the bullet ant's is the mother of all stings!

Folks who have been stung by Central and South American **bullet ants** (*Paraponera clavata*) say the sensation is like being shot by a bullet, and the severe pain, accompanied by trembling of the injured limb, can last for a whole day. In the past, certain South American native people used these ants in initiation ceremonies. Boys would intentionally be stung by the insects. To prove that they were men, they had to show no sign of pain. That's a tough way to say, "I'm a grown-up."

Ants That Spray

Wood ants spraying formic acid.

Wood ants (*Formica*), found on forest floors, and **carpenter ants** (*Camponotus*), which live in dead trees and also buildings, are not stingers—they're sprayers. A spraying ant will grab hold of its prey or enemy with its jaws. Then, depending on the species, it will either tuck its abdomen under its legs or raise it over its back and squirt *formic acid*.

This pungent toxic liquid is powerful stuff. It can repel and even kill animals. But spraying ants usually won't spray unless they're also biting. An ant predator called the **antlion** (*Myrmeleon*) can capture and feed on these ants while preventing them from spraying.

Some species of antlions dig a shallow cone-shaped pit in sand. The antlion then waits at the bottom of the trap for its prey to fall in and attacks before the ant has a chance to bite, and therefore spray. It usually helps the prey slide down the tunnel by flipping sand at the ant with its huge jaws and head. Antlions are also called "doodlebugs" because they make artistic-looking trails in the sand as they search for the best place to dig their pit.

An antlion eating an ant.

Devils in the Garden

Formic acid can also kill plants. In the Amazon rainforest there are areas in which all but one species of plants are dead. They're called "devil's gardens." Some native people believed that evil spirits tended these gardens. Scientists have recently discovered that these spirits are none other than ants—**lemon ants** (*Myrmelachista schumanni*), to be precise. They colonize certain trees, which they prefer for their hollow stems, and spray formic acid as an herbicide to rid their territory of competing plants. One lemon ant garden is more than a third of an acre in size and approximately eight hundred years old.

In the early twentieth century, **yellow crazy ants** (*Anoplolepis gracilipes*) were accidentally introduced on Christmas Island in the Pacific Ocean. Thanks to their formic acid, these insects, named for their frantic movements when disturbed, changed the island's entire ecosystem.

Land crabs used to migrate in great numbers across the land. When they moved through areas infested with the yellow crazy ants, the ants thought the crabs were enemies. The insects sprayed so much formic acid that fifteen to twenty million crabs were blinded and then killed. Seedlings and weeds that used to be eaten by the crabs thrived, displacing other animals and plants. The parks service there has now succeeded in finding a poison that destroys the ants but doesn't harm any other animals, and the island's ecological balance is being restored.

No Soap? Try an Ant Scrub Instead

starling

Formic acid isn't something you'd want to put on your skin, but many species of birds use it on their feathers. Some, such as jays, starlings, and crows, sit on anthills and let the ants swarm over them or actively pick up ants and rub them on their bodies. No one is sure why birds practice *anting*. It is possible that the formic acid kills fleas, lice, and other insects that pester the birds. Another theory is that once the ants discharge their formic acid, they're a tasty snack for the birds.

Snake in the Grass, Alas!

Crawling through fields, meadows, and dry grasslands called *savannahs* is another group of biters and sprayers. To many people, they're the scariest animals of all. They are snakes.

Snakes live in a wide variety of habitats besides savannahs—deserts, rainforests, woodlands, and even your backyard. They come in many colors and lengths, but none of them are slimy. They are *reptiles*—cold-blooded animals with backbones and dry, scaly skin. Some snakes, like other reptiles, lay eggs; others bear live young. All are carnivorous.

It was formerly believed that of the nearly three thousand species of snakes, only three hundred were venomous. But recent research indicates that most snakes can produce venom—although the majority are too small or too shy or are physically unable to inject the venom into us.

a nonvenomous garter snake

a venomous copperhead snake

Which Came First: The Venom or the Snake?

Dr. Bryan Fry, biologist at the University of Melbourne, Australia, says it was venom. He believes that it existed two hundred million years ago—one hundred million years before the first snakes appeared. A common ancestor of snakes and lizards had venom, which it dispensed through its upper and lower jaws. As snakes evolved, each family developed its own venom, a brew of old and new toxins, delivered only through teeth in their upper jaws.

The earliest venomous snakes most likely had enlarged, grooved rear teeth that were located below glands that secreted toxic saliva to help subdue prey. These reptiles were the *opisthoglyphs*—the rear-fanged snakes. Then, according to one theory, the snakes' jaws got smaller, and the rear fangs moved to the front of their mouths. The grooves deepened and connected to form short, fixed hollow tubes. And the *proteroglyphs*—front-fanged snakes—appeared. Eventually these fangs lengthened. In fact, they became so long that snakes could not close their mouths unless they could also fold their fangs, and so the *solenoglyphs* —the vipers—evolved.

Because snake skeletons are fragile, fossil evidence is inconclusive. Newer methods of investigation using DNA may reveal more information about snake evolution.

A diamondback rattlesnake is a front-fanged species.

Why Snakes Drive Us Insane

Ophidiphobia. It means "fear of snakes." People acquire it from parents, other relatives, friends, television, and movies. Or do they? Some scientists think humans have been programmed for millions of years to fear these reptiles. They believe that our mammalian ancestors, who lived in a time when reptiles dominated the world, developed a healthy respect for these critters, and that they genetically passed the fear along to us.

It's true that about fifty thousand people currently die each year from snakebites. But it's also true that as much as we fear snakes, they fear us a lot more. Most are not aggressive, and they prefer to crawl away from, not toward, us. Sad to say, these fascinating animals are persecuted and also hunted for their skins. No wonder they've developed anthropophobia, fear of people.

1 reticulated python

2 black rat snake

3 black mamba

4 inland glass lizard

5 banded sea snake

6 common death adder

7 emerald tree boa

8 green moray eel

How's It Gonna Getcha?

Which three snakes suffocate their prey and which three use venom?

Answers: constrictors: 1, 2, 7; venomous snakes: 3, 5, 6. Number 4 is actually a lizard, and; Number 8 is a fish. Were you fooled?

How Do I Kill Thee? Let Me Count the Ways

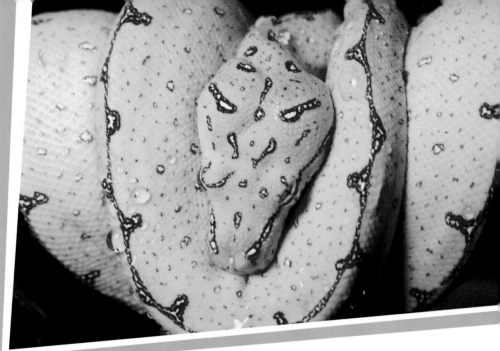

python

Not all snakes use venom to kill their victims. Some snakes use *constriction*—they seize the prey with their small, backward-pointing teeth, then quickly wrap themselves around the victim and tighten their muscles to suffocate it. The most famous of these constrictors are the **pythons** and **boas**.

Like the constrictors, venomous snakes have "regular" teeth to seize prey and to prevent it from slipping out of their mouths, but they also have a pair of hollow fangs in their upper jaws to inject toxins. If a snake loses a fang, another one usually replaces it, sometimes as often as once a week. Baby venomous snakes are born with fangs and the ability to inject venom. They will shed teeth and fangs many times during their lives.

Some snakes bite and hold their prey, chewing to inject venom deep in the wound. Others strike and quickly withdraw. As for a snake's forked tongue, it cannot sting—it is used to taste/smell the air to find food.

Snake venom has to work quickly and efficiently to subdue prey. That's why it is so potent. A struggling victim is dangerous not only when it is caught, but also when it is swallowed. It could easily break the snake's ribs or skull. So the snake waits until the prey is paralyzed, tracks it by smell, and then swallows it. A snake's jaws are connected by stretchy skin and ligaments so it can open its mouth very wide. The two sides of the jaws work independently, "walking" the prey to the rear of the snake's mouth and down its throat.

boa constrictor

fer-de-lance

A snake's venom is actually modified saliva. It is produced in special glands below and behind the snake's eyes, and it flows into tissues surrounding the base of the fangs, and then into the fangs' venom canals. It is mostly made up of proteins in the form of enzymes that help break down the prey quickly. In one study, a venomous snake called a **fer-de-lance** (*Bothrops asper*)—found in Central and South American rainforests, clearings, and fields—had its venom removed. Instead of the two or three days the snake usually needed to digest a rat, it took this snake twelve days.

Studies of *Bothrops* venom have also resulted in the discovery of *beta blockers*—drugs used to treat cardiovascular diseases. In fact, snake venom components are used in many areas of medicine. From cobra venom, scientists have developed several painkillers. Other venoms have produced *anticoagulants* that prevent blood clots. Venoms are currently being investigated for their potential to kill harmful viruses and bacteria and to treat other cardiovascular, nerve, muscular, and joint diseases, as well as visual disorders.

A copperhead uses its fangs and jaws to "walk" its prey (a mouse) toward its throat.

All Kinds of Fangs, Everywhere

Today, all three categories of venomous snakes are still around—the rear-fanged and the two front-fanged types, fixed and folding—and they're found in grasslands, as well as many other habitats, all over the world.

Rear-fanged snakes inject venom as they "chew" their prey. They include the Asian forest-dwelling **green vine snake** (*Ahaetulla nasuta*) and the **African boomslang** (*Dispholidus typus*)

Asian green vine snake

of the savannahs. Most rear-fanged snakes are not as dangerous to humans as front-fanged snakes.

Among the front-fanged snakes with fixed fangs are kraits, sea snakes, brown snakes, taipans, mambas, death adders, and the famous cobras. All of these snakes can bite, but some cobras are also known for their ability to shoot venom through openings in their fangs. They are the **spitting cobras** (example: *Naja nigricollis nigricincta*), many of which are found on the savannahs and grasslands of Africa and Asia. The openings in their fangs are somewhat shorter and rounder than those of non-spitters.

Spitting cobras spray only in self-defense. When a cobra is about to spurt, it rises up, spreads its hood, and aims with great accuracy at an enemy's eyes. The spray can travel more than ten feet to blind the attacker. People who have been sprayed need to flush out their eyes with water immediately to prevent damage. Some scientists believe that this spraying behavior developed as the snakes' way of avoiding being trampled by antelopes, which share the same territory.

To catch prey, a spitting cobra does not spit. It injects neurotoxic venom with its fixed fangs—just like its non-spitting, twelve-to-eighteen-foot cousin, the **Asian king cobra** (*Ophiophagus hannah*), the longest venomous snake in the world.

boomslang snake

Asian king cobra

Cobra venom is very strong indeed, but other fixed-fang snakes have even more powerful venoms. These include the **sea snakes** (example: *Aipysurus laevis*), found in the Pacific and Indian oceans, and the Australian desert-dwelling **inland taipan** (*Oxyuranus microlepidotus*). The venom in one bite of an inland taipan, also called the **fierce snake**, can kill two hundred thousand mice, or approximately sixty-two humans. However, none of these species are aggressive, and they are less likely to encounter people than cobras or *terrestrial* (land-based) **kraits** (example: *Bungarus fasciatus*), which sometimes enter people's homes and are responsible for a great number of *envenomations* and some deaths.

sea snake

How Charming!

The man in the turban sits cross-legged on the ground. In front of him is a closed basket. He removes the lid and begins to play the flute. From the basket, a cobra begins to rise. The snake spreads its hood and sways to and fro to the tune. Then, as if on cue, the snake charmer stops playing and the snake disappears back into its container. Hypnosis? Magic? Uh-uh. Biology!

When the basket cover is removed, the snake is startled by the sudden light and by the charmer waving his flute overhead. It rises defensively, following the movement of the flute with its body. It cannot hear the tune because all snakes are deaf, but it may feel the vibrations. Its "dance" is threatening, but it doesn't attack because it prefers to scare off a possible predator rather than fight or bite. Furthermore, it can't strike upwards, only downwards, and the charmer is probably out of striking range anyway. If it does strike, the charmer doesn't usually suffer severely, perhaps because he has become immune to the venom or because the snake has delivered a dry bite. When the charmer stops waving the flute, the snake no longer needs its threat display, and it retreats to safety and darkness.

Snake charming was once promoted in India and other countries for tourism. But animal rights groups have had an impact on the practice. Most snake charmers treat their animals well, but others are cruel to these reptiles. They remove the venom glands or fangs or even sew shut the snakes' mouths. Today, snake charming is no longer legal, but the Indian government and animal rights groups, along with the charmers, are examining the possibility of the snake handlers becoming reptile rescuers and educators, as well as practitioners who treat cases of snakebite.

Venom
Down Under

Besides the inland taipan and its cousin, the **common taipan** (*Oxyuranus scutellatus scutellatus*), Australia is home to some of the other most venomous snakes in the world. One is the **death adder** (example: *Acanthophis antarcticus*), which tends to stay put when prey, or people, approach. Others include the timid **tiger snake** (*Notechis scutatus*) and the **eastern brown snake** (*Pseudonaja textilis*), which can be found in pastures and farmlands, among other habitats. The latter has been responsible for the most deaths by snakebite in that country—but, thanks to antivenin, that number has been greatly reduced to one or two per year.

The brown snake's venom is twelve times more powerful than a cobra's, and it has a fascinating ingredient: a *procoagulant*, an agent that causes big blood clots to form. After a serious accident or during surgery, it's essential to get blood to clot quickly. Scientists believe that they can eventually create a spray made from the brown snake's procoagulant that can stop bleeding. It seems that this reptile's future is to save rather than take human lives.

common taipan

death adder

brown snake

Mambo, Yes. Mamba, No!

In Africa, another dangerous fixed-fang snake, which sometimes finds its way into folks' homes, is the savannah-dwelling **black mamba** (*Dendroaspis polylepis*). It hunts during the day and is one of the world's fastest-moving snakes. It is at home on both the ground and in the trees, often at the level of a person's head, and it sometimes enters abodes to search for food. It does not seek to bite people, but it will strike to protect itself and its home.

Mamba venom is particularly strong, containing both neuro- and cardiotoxins that affect the nerves and the heart. As little as two drops of its venom can kill a human, and mambas can have as many as twenty drops in their fangs. Fortunately, an available antivenin has significantly reduced the number of human deaths caused by mamba bites.

black mamba

secretary bird

How Do You Take Your Snake Steak?

Many animals prey on young snakes. Some, including people, even feed on full-grown reptiles. (Some folks claim that snake meat tastes like chicken.) The **mongoose** (*Herpestes*) eats a variety of foods, but it is famous for killing African and Asian cobras. This mammal is fast and agile, and its sharp teeth can break a snake's spine. Its thick fur protects it from snakebite, and, though it is not immune to the venom, it probably has a high tolerance to it.

The **secretary bird** (*Sagittarius serpentarius*) also has a varied diet, but it is known as the foe of mambas and other terrestrial African snakes. Named for the feathers on its head that resemble the quill pens that secretaries used to stick behind their ears many years ago, this bird of prey walks up to twenty miles a day in search of food. When it finds a snake, the bird grabs the reptile with its strong toes and stamps on it or beats it to death on the ground, while protecting itself from bites with its large wings.

Snakes feed on other snakes, too. The king cobra is a snake-eater. So is the **American king snake** (Example: *Lampropeltis getula*), found in a wide range of habitats from swamps to deserts. It kills by constriction and is immune to venom, so it can feed on venomous snakes, along with other delicacies, such as lizards, small mammals, and eggs. King snakes have been known to swallow rattlesnakes equal to their own length. That's one large meal!

king snake eating another snake

Vipers!

Vipers are the folding-fang snakes. In Asia, a deadly grassland biter is the **Russell's viper** (*Daboia russelii*). It is responsible for thousands of deaths throughout its range. The Russell's viper is an abundant species that often lives in rice fields, so farmers are sometimes bitten when the rice is being planted and harvested. The toxins affect the kidneys and prevent blood from clotting.

But getting rid of snakes from these fields isn't a good answer. History has shown that in places where snakes have been eliminated, populations of rodents and other vermin explode, and crops, stored grains, and other food get destroyed. Rodents are also carriers of many diseases, so snakes are a good biological control to prevent epidemics.

In both Asia and Africa, one of the most feared terrestrial snakes is the **saw-scaled viper** (*Echis carinatus*), also known as a **carpet viper**. According to *The Guinness Book of World Records*, this species is responsible for more human deaths than any other snake—nearly fifty people per million each year.

Found in a wide variety of environments, this viper has scales on its sides that resemble saw teeth. It warns enemies by rubbing the scales together, making a loud hissing sound like an air leak. The saw-scaled viper is known for its nervous nature, which makes it quicker to attack than most other snakes. Its potent venom is both neurotoxic and hemotoxic.

Russell's viper

saw-scaled viper

In the U.S., more people are bitten by **copperheads** (*Agkistrodon contortrix*) than by other venomous snakes. These terrestrial vipers are the most common venomous snakes in America and are widespread. They live in grassy fields, forests, mountains, and dry lands, as well as by streams and waterways—often near homes and towns. But because their fangs are short and their venom is mild, copperheads kill few people.

In fact, copperheads may soon save many lives. Scientists have isolated a protein called *contortrostatin* in their venom, which shows great promise in stopping both the growth and spread of breast and other cancers.

Fortunately, few people die of snakebites, period, because the venom is meant for much smaller animals. Like spiders, venomous snakes often give people "dry" bites with no venom; they don't want to waste it on animals they can't eat. However, even if you're not a rat or a sparrow, it's still smart to let that snake in the grass quietly pass.

copperhead

What to Do in Case of
Snakebite

1. Get away.

Although it helps to identify the snake, it's more important to avoid further bites by getting the victim away from the animal, so never attempt to capture it.

2. Calm down.

According to the American Red Cross, you should relax the patient and calmly remove any clothing or jewelry from the limb where the bite occurred.

3. Clean up.

Wash the wound with soap and water, but nothing else.

4. Stay still.

Immobilize the limb and keep it lower than the heart to minimize the risk of venom reaching the heart and other organs.

5. Get help.

Get medical help immediately. This is most important, especially if you suspect the snake is venomous. The Red Cross also says that if no medical help is available within thirty minutes, an elastic bandage (or even clothing strips or pantyhose) wrapped around the limb may slow down venom circulation. The bandage should be the same pressure you'd use to wrap a sprain; it should not cut off blood flow.

6. Don't, don't, don't.

No matter what you've seen in fictional movies or TV shows, *never ever* cut the wound; attempt to suck out the venom; use a tourniquet (a tight band to stop bleeding) or electric shock; apply ice to the bite; or give the patient food, drink, or painkillers. These treatments may be harmful, resulting in the loss of a limb or other injuries.

Having a Heat Wave, A *Venomous* Heat Wave

When it comes to venomous critters, many of them like to have their feet (or legs or bellies) on the ground. Some prefer grasslands, but others take to even drier areas—the deserts. These animals include many reptiles, especially snakes and lizards, and among the lizards is a real, live, scaly, pink-and-black monster—the Gila (HEE-lah) monster.

The Healing Gila

A lizard that spends much of its time underground to escape the desert heat, the **Gila monster** (*Heloderma suspectum*) must come out to feed. And when it does, this lizard grabs hold with its teeth and hangs on like a pit bull. Its painful bite can kill its prey—or make a larger enemy like you feel dizzy and weak.

The Gila monster has grooved teeth that are connected to venom glands in its lower jaw. It needs to hold onto a victim and chew in order to deliver its neurotoxic venom. This is a slow method, so scientists believe that the lizard's venom is mainly for self-defense, rather than predation. It is rarely, if ever, fatal to people.

In fact, the venom is now being used to help some people who have diabetes, a disorder in which the body can't control blood sugar because it doesn't produce or properly use the hormone insulin. Patients with this disease sometimes have to inject themselves with the hormone. The problem with injected insulin is that it can make the blood sugar level too low instead of too high. Though the Gila monster eats one big meal and then fasts for months, its blood sugar always stays at

The Gila monster *(above and below)* has venom glands in its lower jaw.

the same level. This fact led Dr. John Eng to investigate the reptile's venom and to discover a hormone that forces blood cells to deal with sugar overload, but stops working when the right sugar level is reached. It also helps diabetics lose weight. The Gila monster drug is already on the market and proving to be highly successful. Dr. Eng and millions of diabetics are giving thanks to one beautiful lizard.

For a long time, the Gila monster, found in the Mojave, Sonoran, and Chihuahuan deserts, and its Latin American cousin, the **Mexican**

Mexican beaded lizard

beaded lizard (*Heloderma horridum*) were thought to be the only venomous lizards in the world. People who have been bitten by other lizards often develop pain, swelling, and prolonged bleeding, but scientists used to think that the cause was the bacteria in the lizards' mouths. However, Dr. Bryan Fry's recent research suggests that **forest-dwelling iguanas** (*Iguana*) and **monitor lizards** (*Varanus*), such as the largest lizard of all, the **Komodo dragon** (*Varanus komodoensis*) of Indonesia, also produce venom, but not in quantities sufficient to harm us seriously. Perhaps the venom is responsible for some of the painful bites—or perhaps it is a combination of venom and bacteria.

You're a Cold-Blooded Snake!

Like all reptiles, lizards and snakes are cold-blooded animals. That means they don't keep a constant body temperature the way birds and mammals do. Desert lizards and snakes need to be warmed by the sun so they can move, digest food, hunt, and mate. But if they were to stay in the sun all day, they'd fry. So these reptiles need to escape into burrows, under rocks, or beneath the sand when the air gets too hot. Many hunt at night when it's cooler, and then catch some rays in the morning before hiding out during the hottest hours of the day.

Komodo dragons

Are You Feeling Rattled?

Lizards don't have fangs to inject venom quickly and efficiently, but **desert rattlesnakes** (*Crotalus*) do. Like copperheads, rattlesnakes are pit vipers—they have heat-sensing openings between their eyes and nostrils to detect prey. In addition, like many snakes, they use camouflage to hide from prey. But camouflage can be a problem when big enemies appear. So these snakes shake their rattles to warn horses, cattle, people, and other large animals not to step on them. If the rattling doesn't work, then they strike, injecting hemotoxic venom that destroys tissues and organs and disrupts blood clotting. It isn't true that they must coil into an S-shape to strike, and they can lunge almost faster than the human eye can see.

Many snakes lay eggs, but rattlers give birth to live young. The babies have short fangs, but are venomous and dangerous—perhaps even more dangerous than adults. They don't have rattles to warn enemies, so when disturbed, they immediately become defensive and may strike repeatedly. Though they produce less venom, it appears to have a higher concentration of toxins. In addition, young snakes haven't yet learned what is and is not

rattlesnake

a serious threat, and they tend to deliver a full dose rather than a dry bite.

Rattlesnake bites from babies or adults are always serious, and sometimes fatal, though anti-venins have significantly reduced deaths from them.

Rattlesnakes have many non-venomous mimics. **Gopher snakes** (*Pituophis melanoleuces*), **rat snake**, (*Elaphe*) and **racers** (Example: *Coluber constrictor*) vibrate their rattle-less tails in dry grass or leaves to make rattle-like sounds. From their underground homes, **burrowing owls** (*Athene cunicularia*) make rattling hisses that have fooled folks into thinking they're reptiles, not birds.

Snakes and lizards are found in a wide variety of habitats, but they are often associated with the desert. So are tarantulas and scorpions.

gopher snake

rat snake

burrowing owl

Loop-De-Loop

Deserts are regions with very little rainfall. They cover one-fifth of the earth's surface. Some are cool places that may even have snowfall in winter, but we're most familiar with the deserts that are hot, such as the American Mojave or the African Sahara. Because of the burning, shifting sands, it's hard for animals to travel across the desert. One type of rattlesnake that has found a solution is the **American sidewinder** (*Crotalus cerastes*). This species of rattlesnake loops sideways over the dunes, with just two spots of its body touching the sand at any one time. Using this unique locomotion, the sidewinder can move quickly to prey on rodents, lizards, and sometimes birds, leaving a series of J-shaped tracks in the sand.

Sidewinders have "horns"—scales that stick out over their eyes to protect them from grit as they enter their underground burrows. Some Saharan and other desert snakes also have these horns and use the side-winding motion to travel.

American sidewinder

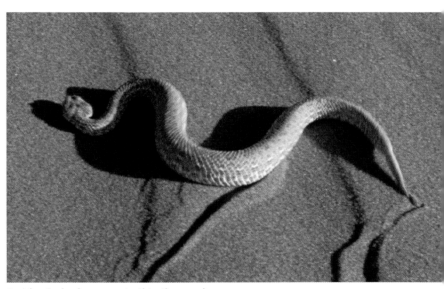
A sidewinder leaves a trail in the sand.

Which Part of the Scorpion Delivers the Venom?

A pedipalps

B chelicerae

C aculeus

D mesosoma

E legs

F earlobes

answer on the next page!

Desert 47

Poison Part

If you answered *C*, you're right! The *aculeus* is the stinger at the end of the scorpion's *telson*—the last, fat segment of its long tail-like abdomen where its venom glands are found. The *pedipalps* are its huge claws or pincers. The *chelicerae* are its mouthparts—but, unlike a spider's, a scorpion's chelicerae don't end in fangs.

The *mesosoma* is the main part of its body. (The *metasoma* is the entire tail section.) The scorpion has eight harmless legs—and no earlobes whatsoever.

Parts of a Scorpion

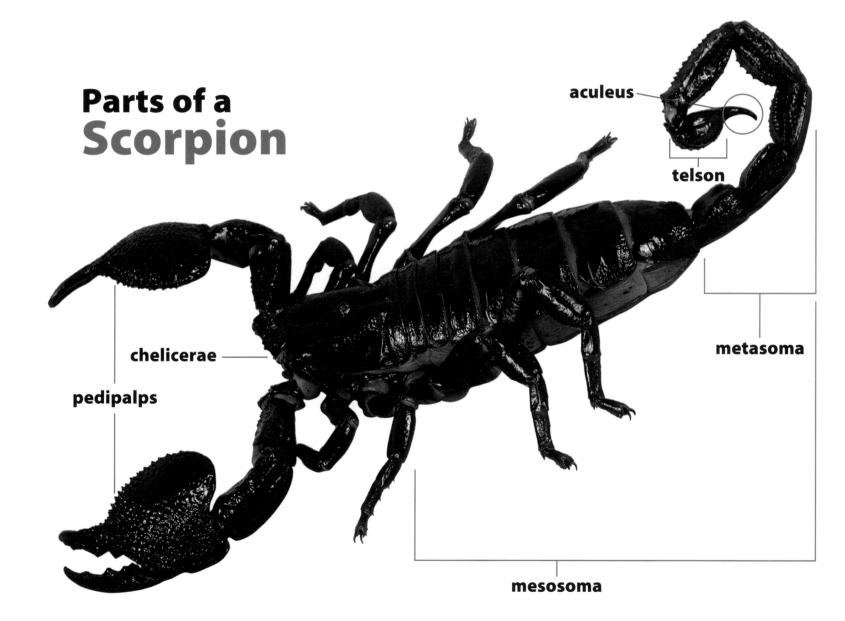

aculeus

telson

metasoma

chelicerae

pedipalps

mesosoma

The Sign of the Scorpion

Scorpions are nocturnal arachnids that glow in the dark. They use their pincers to grab insects, worms, lizards, mice, and other scorpions. They inject neurotoxic venom into their prey, as well as their enemies, with stingers on their rear ends. Recent research indicates that some, and perhaps all, **scorpions** (example: *Parabuthus transvaalicus*) have a thick venom and a thinner *prevenom*.

Venom is made up mostly of protein, and it requires a lot energy to produce. Scorpions need venom to subdue larger, more dangerous prey or to escape from enemies that won't leave them alone. Prevenom has less protein and requires less energy to make. It works against smaller, non-threatening species—and it causes greater pain. A mouse that receives a dose of prevenom will jump around, then stop to nurse its injected limb, giving the scorpion a chance to get away. Scientists now want to study other venomous animals to see if they, too, produce prevenom.

Eons ago some scorpions were huge—three feet long! Now the largest one, the **emperor scorpion** (*Pandinus imperator*) of North Africa, is only eight inches long—still big, but not gigantic. But these large emperors rarely sting people. In fact, they are sometimes kept as pets—and unfortunately, over-collecting is responsible for their decline in the wild.

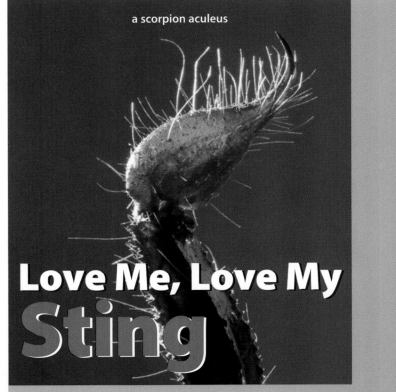

a scorpion aculeus

Love Me, Love My Sting

When scorpions mate, they seem to dance. The male, who is smaller, grasps the female's pedipalps and leads her around, sometimes for as long as an hour. During the dance, a male may sting a female. No one is sure why, but the most likely reason is that he needs to subdue her and make sure she doesn't eat him while they mate.

emperor scorpion

Far more dangerous to people are the two-inch-long **bark scorpions** (*Centruroides exilicauda*), the only deadly scorpion species in the U.S., and the two- to four-inch-long **Sahara scorpions** (example: *Androctonus australis*), which are probably the deadliest scorpions in the world. Scorpions with big, strong pincers, such as the emperors, usually rely on grabbing and eating their prey instead of envenoming it first. The deadly species have narrower and weaker pincers.

Despite their venom, scorpions are eaten by lizards, mongooses, burrowing owls, and other animals. These predators bite or break off the scorpion's metasoma first. This just goes to prove that in the desert—and everywhere else—poison only works if you get a chance to use it.

bark scorpion

Sahara scorpion

Is This Scorpion for Real?

A **water scorpion** (*Ranatra*) isn't a scorpion at all. It's a venomous insect. It has pincer-like forelegs for seizing prey, and its "tail" is actually a siphon—a kind of snorkel to get air while the bug is underwater, where it hunts other insects, shrimp, and worms. It can't sting you because it has no stinger, but it can give one nasty venomous bite through its sharp rostrum, so handle with care.

All A-Glow

Scientists and other folks who are interested in scorpions can find them at night in their natural habitats by using handheld black lights that produce ultraviolet (UV) light. When exposed to this light, scorpions *fluoresce*. A thin, transparent film called *hyaline* found in their *cuticle*—the outermost layer of their exoskeleton—contains a special protein that allows them to glow green-blue or green-yellow in the dark. When scorpions *molt*—shed their exoskeleton as they grow—they do not glow until their new cuticle hardens.

Why *do* they glow? Scientists are not sure. One theory is that scorpions can see fluorescence without the aid of UV light and, therefore, they can find or avoid each other. But some scientists doubt the ability of these arachnids to see the glow. Another theory is that there are other nocturnal predators capable of detecting this fluorescence, allowing them to spot and stay away from these venomous arachnids.

A Cure from the Desert

Doctors have created a synthetic version of a protein found in the venom of the **giant yellow Israeli scorpion** or **death stalker** (*Leiurus quinquestriatus*) to fight a type of brain tumor. The protein can deliver radioactive iodine, a chemotherapy agent, directly to the cancerous cells to kill them while leaving the healthy cells alone. It might also have cancer-fighting properties itself. As one doctor said, "Using radioactive scorpion venom sounds like science fiction," but it is actually science fact! Medical trials are so promising that doctors now want to see if the protein works against other tumors, as well.

giant yellow Israeli scorpion

Poisoners in the Pond

The old swimming hole. For many folks, it's the spot where they skate in the winter, cool off in the summer, and fish most of the year. For other critters, it's the place to feed and breed. And since poisonous and venomous critters can be found most anywhere, you can bet your bathing suit that some of these pond dwellers are toxic.

Can You Touch Your Toads?

Toad tadpoles. Some insects will eat them, but many other animals won't. Why? Because they're poisonous.

Toads (example: *Bufo americanus*) are amphibians—cold-blooded animals with backbones that are generally born in moist places. They live in forests and deserts, as well as in and near freshwater ponds and streams. As tadpoles, or larvae, amphibians need gills to breathe, and then they develop into adults with lungs and legs. Some species spend their entire lives in water. Others, such as many types of toads, are more terrestrial. But they still need to lay their eggs in ponds and other damp areas.

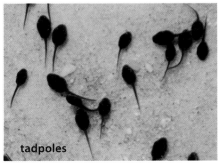
tadpoles

The Truth about TOADS

True or False?

1 Toads give you warts.

2 Toads may pee on you if you pick them up.

3 Toads inject venom with their teeth.

4 Toads have toxins in their skin.

5 Toads can puff up to repel predators.

Answers: 1. False; 2. True. They do that to be unappetizing to predators; 3. False. They are not venomous, and they don't even have teeth, but frogs do; 4. True; 5. True.

Frog vs Toad

frog

toad

What is the difference between a frog and a toad? Technically, toads *are* frogs, and it is often hard to distinguish one from another. But while true frogs (members of the Ranidae family) have smooth, moist skin and long hind legs with webbed feet, true toads (members of the Bufonidae family) have dry, bumpy skin and short hind legs. And unlike their North American frog cousins, North American toads are poisonous at all stages of their life cycle: egg, tadpole, and adult.

Toad poison is a fluid produced from large *parotid glands* behind the animal's eyes and from glands on its back. The fluid tastes terrible and will burn a predator's mouth, eyes, and skin. Depending on the species, the toad's poison ranges from irritating to deadly. Some species, such as the **fire-bellied toads** (*Bombina*) of Europe and Asia, are aposematic, advertising their toxins by arching their backs and rais-

parotid glands

ing both their front and hind legs to display their red- or yellow-and-black bellies.

All toads are hunters. They eat fish, worms, slugs, spiders, birds, mice, and especially insects, which makes them welcome to gardeners and farmers. But one toad has become more of a nuisance than a friend—and humans have only themselves to blame for the problem. It's the **cane** or **marine toad** (*Bufo marinus*).

Hedgehogs Love Toad Venom

Hedgehogs are cute critters with non-venomous, non-barbed spines. They defend themselves by rolling into a prickly ball. These mammals, found in Europe, Asia, Africa, and New Zealand, often *self-anoint*—

they smear their spines with various substances. For some species, one of those substances is toad poison. The hedgehog will chew toad skin and then lick its spines to coat them with the saliva-poison mixture. It may use the poison in self-defense, for getting rid of parasites, for attracting a mate, or for all those (and other) reasons.

This Cane Is a Pain

Indigenous to Central and South America, the cane toad lives mainly on land, but it breeds in fresh water. It can spray, as well as ooze, its heart-stopping poison. In its native habitats, the cane toad population has been kept in check by predators, which include fish, caimans, and snakes. But in Australia, this amphibian has become a serious pest.

cane toad

Up until 1935, Australia had no toads at all. Some people thought it would be a good idea to bring in a species that would eat sugar cane pests: **greyback** and **French's cane beetles** (*Dermolepida albohirtum* and *Lepidiota frenchi*). They selected the cane toad, which had been introduced in Hawaii and was doing well in that climate. Unfortunately, the toads failed to eat the beetles. Instead, they bred and bred and bred some more and began to eat other critters, including Australia's native frogs.

But few critters could eat the cane toads and survive. Fish that ate their tadpoles died. Other animals, including crocodiles and pet dogs, that dined on the adult toads died, too. The **northern quoll** (*Dasyurus hallucatus*), a carnivorous marsupial, has now become severely endangered, not only because of habitat loss, but also because of cane toad poisoning. A recent study says that several snakes are evolving defenses against the toads. They are developing smaller heads and longer bodies, which means that they can't swallow the cane toads—they can take only smaller and safer prey.

Other Australian predators, such as a few varieties of turtles and snakes, can tolerate the toad's toxins. Some species of birds and rats, have adapted to eat only the toad's nontoxic tongue or have learned to flip the toad, attack its belly, and devour its internal organs.

Unfortunately, there aren't enough predators to eat enough of the toads. And the diseases and parasites that control the toad population in other countries aren't found in Australia. Then there's the stunning fact that each pair of toads can produce as many as thirty-five thousand eggs twice a year. That's a lot of toads—and a lot of toad toxin. Australia is currently spending millions of dollars to find biological controls to deal with the species. Environmentalists have even recently asked the country's military to wage war on them in an effort to stop their spread.

Snake in the Grass
...er...Pond

Some snakes, such as **hognose** (*Heterodon*) and **water snakes** (*Nerodia*), are immune to toad poison and can eat adult toads. Hognose snakes are mildly venomous to people. Water snakes are not known to be venomous, but people sometimes confuse them with a snake that is— the **cottonmouth** (*Agkistrodon piscivorus*), also known as the **water moccasin**.

hognose snake

The cottonmouth is the only venomous aquatic snake in America. It is rarely found far from a water source—a pond, a lake, a slow-moving stream, a swamp, or an *estuary* (an area where freshwater and seawater mix). Although this snake has a bad reputation, it is not aggressive. When it's threatened, it will try to escape or it will "gape," opening its mouth wide to show the white lining, which is how it got its name. If the enemy does not back off, it may bite with its long fangs to inject powerful hemotoxic venom.

However, it mostly uses this venom to kill prey such as fish, frogs, and mice, and the toxins are rarely strong enough to be fatal to humans. A cottonmouth will never feast on toads. That dinner might very well be its last.

cottonmouth snake

Beware of the
Toe Biters

The cottonmouth might not munch on toads, but **backswimmers** (Notonecta glauca) and **giant water bugs** (*Lethocerus americanus*) feed on a variety of water creatures including tadpoles. Backswimmers paddle upside-down on the surface of ponds. Water bugs lie in wait underwater, clinging to plants or sticks, using a snorkel-like tube at the tip of their abdomen to get oxygen. When they spot prey, both species use their sharp rostrums to inject venom into a victim and suck out its juices. Giant water bugs are known as "toe-biters" because if you dangle your feet into their territory, they can give you a painful bite.

Backswimmers and water bugs have wings, and you may be more likely to encounter the latter when they're flying around outdoors, especially near electric lights, on their way to find a new pond or stream in which to mate.

backswimmer

giant water bug with prey

Stopping by the Woods on a Toxic Evening

Whose woods these are I think I know . . . toxic critters there, below!

With their coolness, moisture, ample food supply, and many places to hide, temperate woodlands and forests are ideal habitats for many animals. Some, such as deer and game birds, are hunted for food. Others, such as many amphibians, are found on no one's menu—and for a good reason: They're pure poison.

Never Swallow a Salamander

Some of those amphibians are toads. Others are newts and salamanders. Actually, a newt is a salamander—but a salamander isn't always a newt. Salamanders are found in a variety of habitats. They may be entirely aquatic, or they may be terrestrial—though, in that case, they still generally need moisture in which to lay eggs, or the eggs themselves have to be moist inside for the larvae to spend their aquatic stage in them. Some salamanders lay eggs on dry land, but then the eggs don't hatch until spring rains submerge them. Newts always breed in water, but they spend the rest of the year on land, so they're called semi-aquatic.

common newt

Like toads and certain frogs, newts and salamanders secrete poison through their scaleless skin. In addition, as a defense, some newts have sharp ribs that poke through their back. The ribs can jab a predator's mouth and also deliver more of the toxin.

Salamander and newt poison ranges from mild to lethal. The **American rough-skin newt** (*Taricha granulosa*) is one of the most toxic animals known to science. It produces *tetrodotoxin*,

rough-skin newt

red-spotted newt

a deadly neurotoxin that blocks signals from the brain that tell an animal's lungs how to breathe and its heart how to beat. Although this poison is the newt's defense against shore birds, bullfrogs, fish, and other predators, it has also been known to hurt and even kill people.

In one case, a scientist had a wound on his finger. He handled a newt, and the toxin entered the cut. He suffered from nausea, dizziness, and a totally numb arm for half an hour. In another far worse incident, a man swallowed a rough-skin newt on a dare. Within ten minutes, his lips began to tingle. During the next two hours, he became weak and numb, and then, despite hospital treatment, his heart stopped and he died. It's best not to handle this amphibian—and, for goodness sake, don't ever swallow one!

Many newts and salamanders are aposematic. Some, like young **red-spotted newts** (*Notophthalmus viridescens*), which are called **red efts**, walk boldly through the eastern American woods, displaying their brilliant red-orange skin to warn predators of their poison. Others, such as the **western red-bellied newt** (*Taricha rivularis*), curve their heads and legs over their backs to display their scarlet undersides when they're threatened—much as red-bellied toads do.

European fire salamanders (*Salamandra salamandra*) not only have poisonous black and yellow skin, but they also can spray toxins from glands on their backs. These amphibians can tilt their bodies in an enemy's direction and spray farther than six feet.

Some predators can see these warning colors, but others can't, so newts and salamanders also wave their heads or tails and make sounds to warn enemies. One woodland critter that has learned to recognize these movements and noises and so avoid noshing on newts is the **short-tailed shrew** (*Blarina brevicauda*), the only venomous mammal in North America—and one of the few venomous mammals in the world.

common salamander

fire salamander

There's No Taming *This* Shrew

Shrews are tiny, solitary, mostly nocturnal animals found in temperate forests throughout most of the world. Fierce predators, they eat many kinds of animals, including insects, earthworms, spiders, birds, amphibians, and rodents (which are sometimes larger than the shrew itself), as well as vegetation, nuts, and fruits.

When a shrew bites its prey, toxic saliva flows through grooves in its lower front teeth to kill or paralyze the victim. Shrews use a lot of energy, so they must eat constantly. They store piles of live, paralyzed prey in their burrows so they'll always have plenty of fresh food on hand.

Although a shrew is immune to its own venom, it probably is not immune to the venom of fellow shrews. These little carnivores are known for feuding over territory. So if a shrew gets bitten by another shrew during a turf war, it may become paralyzed or die.

If you were to get chomped by a shrew, you'd experience pain and swelling, but you'd be unlikely to expire. In fact, shrew venom may be used in the future to help treat migraines, high blood pressure, and neuromuscular diseases, and even to smooth out wrinkles.

Shrews are eaten by owls, hawks, weasels, snakes, and salamanders, but other predators won't touch them. That's not because of their venom. It's because of their stink. A shrew's scent glands make it smell and taste mighty bad. So if your cat leaves a shrew on your doorstep, Felix may well be telling you, "P-U!"

northern short-tailed shrew

More Endangered Than
Dangerous

In Haiti, the Dominican Republic, and Cuba, **solenodons** (*Solenodon paradoxus* and *Solenodon cubanus*) are large cousins of shrews, and, like them, they have venomous saliva and a bad odor. Solenodons tend to be nervous and will squeal and bite readily, but they are much more endangered than dangerous. They have been nearly wiped out by introduced species, such as dogs, cats, and mongooses, which were brought to the islands to hunt mice and rats. Solenodons may even be extinct in some areas.

Who Needs **Speed** When You've Got **Poison?**

Like humans, the **slow loris** (*Nycticebus coucang*) is a primate. It has five strong, gripping fingers with nails on each hand, opposable thumbs (they can touch the other fingers), three kinds of teeth, and a well-developed brain, among other characteristics. The slow loris lives in rainforests and other woodlands, as well as in suburban gardens, where it spends its days sleeping in the trees and its nights searching for fruit, eggs, insects, and other small prey to eat. It moves slowly and deliberately hand-over-hand, though it can climb quickly if startled. It's such an adorable critter, with its big eyes and tiny ears—who would guess it's toxic? Dr. Bryan Fry *knows* it's toxic. After having been bitten several times by these animals, he's discovered that slow lorises secrete toxin from tissues similar to sweat pores on the inside of their elbows. The animals take the toxin into their mouths and deliver it with their saliva when they bite in self-defense. Fry says it appears that mother lorises also comb this toxin through their babies' fur, possibly as protection from predators. There's much to be learned about this mysterious new mammalian poison, and it suggests that more toxic animals may be out there than we could ever have imagined.

A slow loris adult

Dr. Bryan Fry with a slow loris

In the Jungle, the Mighty Jungle, the TOXIC Sleep Tonight

In these forests, something's always singing in the rain. Tropical rainforests are warm, humid belts of green with much rainfall, more than eighty inches annually. All that moisture makes for lush trees, flowers, and fruits—food and home for more than half of the world's animals. Some of them live on the forest floor; others live in various levels of the trees. Some are well camouflaged; others are boldly colored. Let's visit some of the flashy inhabitants first and see what they're announcing.

Pitohui? *Ptooey!*

Shhh. We're in a New Guinea rainforest, where agarwood trees grow, birdwing butterflies glow, and poisonous birds flourish. You don't believe me? Ask a local resident, and he'll point out a pretty, red-and-black creature nicknamed a "rubbish bird." Ask a scientist, and he'll tell you it's a *Pitohui dichrous*—a **hooded pitohui** (PIT-a-hooey). Whatever the name, one taste and you'd go "ptooey," too.

The scientist who first documented the poisonous bird was Jack Dumbacher. In 1989, he caught a hooded pitohui, and, as he was removing it from the net, it bit and scratched his hands. He put a finger in his mouth, and his lips and tongue went numb. From talking to the locals, he discovered that the species was toxic.

hooded pitohui

blue-capped ifrita

The hooded and two other pitohui species, as well as another bird, the **blue-capped ifrita** (*Ifrita kowaldi*), are the only known toxic birds—so far. They have cardio- and neurotoxins called *batrachotoxins* in their feathers and skin that make them smell and taste terrible. Recently, Avit Wako, a New Guinean naturalist, seems to have discovered the source of the toxins: tiny **Melyrid beetles** (example: *Choresine pulchra*), which the birds eat. If tasted, both the birds and the beetles cause people to have burning, tingling sensations in their mouths.

Melyrid beetle

America's Own
Toxic Birds

Once upon a time, brightly colored, native parakeets lived all over the eastern U.S. They were called **Carolina parakeets** (*Conuropsis carolinensis*), and they traveled in huge, noisy flocks of sometimes as many as one thousand birds. But by the early twentieth century, the species went extinct. No one is sure what caused this sad event. Theories include loss of habitat, over-hunting, and disease, or a combination of all of these. Some experts feel that disease was the primary factor, and it revolved around the birds' favorite food, cockleburs.

The cocklebur is a weed that grows in cleared areas around homes and farms. It is toxic to domestic animals, but the parakeets were able to eat the plant with no ill effects. People appreciated the birds' diet because it reduced the weeds and protected their livestock. Several naturalists described how the toxins protected the parakeets, too, by killing animals that tried to eat them.

But as settlements spread, so did cockleburs. When the birds visited the communities to feed on the plants, they were exposed to more and more diseases that are carried by livestock. Because the birds weren't immune to these diseases, they died.

America may indeed have had its own species of toxic birds. It is unfortunate that none of us will ever get to see one.

You Wouldn't Want *This* Frog in Your Throat

Melyrid beetles are also found across the globe in Central and South American rainforests. There, they are the diet of poison dart frogs—and they're the reason some varieties of these little, jewel-colored amphibians, as well as the pitohui and ifrita, are poisonous. If the frogs are removed from their habitat and are fed nontoxic insects, their toxicity lessens. Frogs born and raised in captivity and fed on nonpoisonous bugs never become poisonous at all.

In the wild, poison dart frogs are much more toxic than poisonous birds. In fact, the **golden poison dart frog** (*Phyllobates terribilis*) is one of the most poisonous animals in the world. This tiny amphibian has enough batrachotoxin in its skin to kill twenty thousand mice—or at least eight human beings—if they were to eat the toxin or absorb enough of it through a wound. A lethal

poison dart frog

dose of this poison for a 150-pound person is 136 micrograms—the equivalent of two or three grains of salt! But according to medical studies, poison dart frog toxins may also turn out to be useful as antibiotics and painkillers, substances that cure rather than kill.

All poison dart frogs are aposematic, so most predators know to avoid them. But the Choco people, South American natives of Columbian rainforests, have learned to catch the frogs and collect their venom. They rub it on the darts they use to hunt birds, monkeys, and other animals—which is how the frogs got their familiar name. The poison kills the prey, but doesn't hurt the hunters who eat the meat.

green poison dart frog

blue poison dart frog

Slithering
in the Trees

On the rainforest floor, the golden poison dart frog and its relatives use their colors to announce that they're toxic. Is this Costa Rican **golden eyelash viper** (*Bothriechis schlegelii*) doing the same?

golden eyelash viper

Nope. Would you believe that its daring color is actually camouflage? This nocturnal, venomous snake—named for the scales above its eyes—rests in trees among flowers, fruit, and leaves, hiding from predators. A type of pit viper, the eyelash viper is plentiful in banana groves, where it blends in perfectly. Throughout its range in Central and South America, the snake shows a wide variety of colors, all designed to merge with its surroundings.

Many species of snakes are found in rainforests. The best-known ones are the non-venomous **boas** and **anacondas** (*Eunectes murinus*). But along with the eyelash viper, there are many

anaconda

emerald tree boa

venomous varieties. Some, such as the rear-fanged vine snakes, are *arboreal*—they live up in the trees—and eat lizards, small mammals, and baby birds. They must wrap around their prey and chew for several seconds or even minutes to inject their venom. Most are not dangerous to people.

bushmaster

The **Gaboon viper** (*Bitis gabonica*) of African forests, coastal dunes, and other areas is the heaviest of all vipers, and it produces the most venom. It's also in the record books as the snake with the longest fangs—up to two inches in length. Its colors camouflage it among the leaf litter, where it lies waiting to catch large rodents, ground birds, and other prey. Like some of its relatives, this viper can inflate its body and then deflate it with a hissing sound to threaten predators.

Other snakes, such as the Central and South American **fer-de-lance** and the **bushmaster** (*Lachesis muta*), are terrestrial, living under leaves or in logs on the ground. Like the eyelash viper (and the American cottonmouth and the copperhead), both the fer-de-lance and the bushmaster are pit vipers. These nocturnal snakes have long fangs and potent hemotoxic venom. The fer-de-lance feeds on rodents, lizards, and frogs and is probably responsible for more human deaths in South America than any other snake. The bushmaster, which can grow to twelve feet, making it the longest venomous snake in the Americas, is one of the few snakes to eat only mammals. While the fer-de-lance can live around farms and homes, the bushmaster is found only in undisturbed rainforests, so people are much less likely to encounter it.

Gaboon viper

fer-de-lance

Red Touching Yellow *Kills* a Fellow

Most coral snakes are found in tropical forests—but the American species, the only terrestrial fixed-fang snakes in the U.S., also live in woodlands and in dry, desert-like areas. They have strong neurotoxic venom, but they are not aggressive and their fangs are small, so bites are rare. However, because they're so pretty, kids sometimes pick them up and get bitten.

Coral snakes (example: *Micrurus fulvius*) have several harmless mimics, such as the **scarlet king snake** (*Lampropeltis triangulum*). The way to tell them apart inspired this rhyme: "Red touching yellow kills a fellow/ Red touching black is a friend of Jack." It refers to the bands of color on the snakes. Have a look. Can you tell which is venomous?

This rhyme actually applies mainly to the North American species. Many of the tropical coral snakes with red touching black are NOT friends of Jack. They're venomous. So, whatever bands of color are touching, don't *you* touch any of these snakes!

Wherever It Wanders, Get Out of Its Way!

Snakes are not the only fanged creatures in rainforests. Spiders lurk there, too, including some varieties of tarantulas, funnel-webs, and one of the most venomous spiders in the world: the **Brazilian wandering spider** (*Phoneutria*). This dangerous arachnid can inflict a very painful, neurotoxic bite. It gets its name from the fact that it travels forest floors to catch prey instead of building a web.

But this spider journeys in more ways than one. It has been known to hide in fruit and to hitch rides to countries far from home. In 2005, a chef in Bridgwater, England, was bitten by a wandering spider that had stowed away in a box of bananas. Before he passed out, he snapped a photo of the arachnid with his camera phone—and that picture saved his life. Doctors at the local hospital sent the picture to the Bristol Zoo, where experts identified the five-inch-long spider and told them which anti-venin to give the man. It took a week, but the chef did recover.

coral snake *(left)*, scarlet king snake *(right)*

Up a Lazy River, How Toxic They'll Be!

Rivers run through rainforests, as well as deserts, mountains, plains, and cities. Some flow quickly; others are slow. They carry boats, barges, logs, and, of course, a variety of venomous animals, such as this strange critter . . .

Is It a Bird, Is It a Plane . . . Er . . . What Is It?

It has webbed feet and a bill like a duck, lives by Australian rivers, and lays eggs. But it isn't a bird. Can you name this critter?

That's right—it's a **platypus** (*Ornithorhynchus anatinus*), a semi-aquatic mammal. Found in a wide variety of Australian habitats from snowy highland woods to steamy rainforests, it swims the rivers and streams looking for food. Its sensitive bill has receptors to read electrical currents, which allow the animal to judge its distance from prey and to distinguish insect larvae, freshwater shrimp, and crayfish from nonliving objects. A platypus can stay underwater for ten minutes or so without surfacing. When it isn't hunting, it rests in its burrow in the riverbank.

The platypus, along with three species of **echidnas** (*Zaglossus*)—spiny anteaters found in Australia and New Guinea—are *monotremes*, the only egg-laying mammals on Earth. Echidnas are not venomous. But the male platypus is. Unlike shrews, his toxins aren't in his saliva. They're in his thighs.

The venom glands in a male platypus's legs are connected to hollow spurs on his hind feet. To inject venom, the platypus kicks its legs and jabs the spurs. Some scientists think that these spurs are used both in self-defense and in fighting off other males when the platypuses are looking for mates. The venom can cause pain and swelling in people, so it's not a good idea to try to break up a platypus fight. Let those platypuses work things out for themselves.

A male platypus with a close-up of a spur on its hind foot

Cats and Scats

Platypuses may be the least familiar creatures found in rivers. What are the *most* familiar? Fish. Rivers are home to many kinds of fish: sharp-toothed carnivores, such as **red-bellied piranhas** (*Pygocentrus nattereri*) in the Amazon, vegetarian **grass carp** (*Ctenopharyngodon idella*) in the Amur, and other more common species, such as catfish, in the Mississippi.

With their smooth skin and *barbels*—whiskers—these "cats" may look harmless. But as any

gar

catfish

catfish fisherman can tell you, they have weapons to protect themselves: sharp spines in the fins on both their back and sides. In some catfish species, these spines are venomous.

The **madtom** (*Noturus*) found in some rivers in the U.S. can give you a nasty bee-like sting. The smallest species, the **tadpole madtom** (*Noturus gyrinus*) has the most painful sting of all. But, like most catfish, it will zap you only when trapped or handled. Its Asian riverine cousin, the **Indian catfish** (*Heteropneustes fossilis*), will attack any enemy that enters its territory—and its sting also hurts. The brightly striped **marine catfish** (*Plotosus lineatus*), found in oceans and estuaries, is equally toxic.

Catfish—and the majority of other animals—are most venomous when they are fully grown. However, **scats** (*Scatophagus argus*), which are found in estuaries, harbors, and the lower parts of rivers, are most venomous when they are babies. The youngsters can give mild stings with their spines.

Youngsters are easy prey for many predators, so being a toxic baby makes sense. Eggs are also prey. So some animals lay eggs that are poisonous. Just ask a North American

scat

gar (example: *Atractosteus spatula*). The adult fish, however, is not venomous at all. It doesn't need to be. Its armor-like scales and sharp teeth are plenty of protection against almost any enemy.

Ichthyologists (fish scientists) used to think there were only about two hundred species of venomous fish. Now Dr. William Leo Smith and Ward C. Wheeler of the American Museum of National History believe that there may be more than a thousand. However, most of them do not live in freshwater. They're found in oceans and seas, especially in the Indo-Pacific. A few species have been in American waters for a long time—but a few others have recently arrived. Let's take a swim and meet some of them.

By the Sea, By the Sea, By the Venomous Sea

Wading in the ocean—is it a treat for your feet or a threat to get them wet? The answer might be both! *Venomous fishes often lie in the shallow water near the shore, waiting to catch a meal. They are often well camouflaged to surprise prey, but they sometimes succeed in surprising unsuspecting waders as well. Many stings occur when people accidentally step on these creatures. That's certainly the case with stingrays.*

You Don't Want to Catch These Rays!

Relatives of sharks, rays are flat-bodied fish that have *cartilage*—dense connective tissue—instead of bones. They swim with a flying motion of their large, wing-like pectoral fins. Not all rays are stingrays, but all stingrays have stingers.

The stinger is a long, jagged spine. It can be clipped off, like a fingernail, and it will grow back. It has two grooves filled with venom-producing tissue, and it is surrounded by a sheath that may also produce venom. Stingray venom is neurotoxic, and anyone who is "stung" should seek medical attention.

Stingrays are common in coastal waters throughout the world. There are some freshwater species, such as the **mottled stingray** (*Potamotrygon hystrix*) of the Amazon, but most are ocean dwellers, including the **southern stingray** (*Dasyatis americana*) of the Caribbean.

stingray

Some rays are *benthic*—they spend most of their time resting in the shallows, feeding on worms, clams, shrimp, crabs, snails, and occasionally fish. Benthic rays have spines at the ends of their long "tails." Others are *pelagic*—open water swimmers. The barbs of pelagic rays are close to their bodies, probably to protect their organs in case they are bitten as they swim.

Rays are generally peaceful animals. They will use their spines only if they are stepped on or otherwise threatened—and then they can lash out forcefully to protect themselves. A large ray can exert enough power to drive its barb into a wooden boat. Most injuries occur when a person steps directly on a ray, so waders are advised to shuffle—not stomp—their feet in waters where benthic stingrays lurk. That will usually make the rays swim out of the way.

At the Great Barrier Reef, Steve Irwin, the Australian naturalist nicknamed the "Crocodile Hunter," was killed by a **bull ray**'s (*Dasyatis*

blue-spotted stingray

brevicaudata) stinger—but not by its venom. The ray's barb pierced his heart, and he died almost instantly after pulling it out. A stingray's sting is painful, but it is rarely fatal. The strange thing is, according to *The Australian News*, Irwin was apparently searching for another creature that *is* deadly—the **reef stonefish**.

The Deadliest "Rock" in the World

The reef stonefish (*Synanceia verrucosa*) is a benthic fish that lives on reefs, often under rocks or ledges, in sandy shallows, and in mud flats. Squat, lumpy, and usually dark-colored—though sometimes splashed with pink or red—the fish lies there, looking like a rock or a piece of coral. With this camouflage, it can fool prey. When small fishes and shrimp unknowingly swim by, the stonefish opens its mouth and, in a flash, swallows them.

Enemies may be fooled, too. But if they get too close, the stonefish erects its toxic defense: thirteen venomous spines along its back. These spines can pierce right through the bottom of sneakers and flippers. Each spine has enough venom to kill one thousand mice and it can be fatal to people. Pressing on the spines releases the toxins, which cause excruciating pain, swelling, tissue destruction,

muscle weakness, paralysis, shock, and sometimes death by heart failure. There is now an antivenin to treat these severe stings.

reef stonefish

Saltwater Snakes

banded sea kraits

The stonefish has few natural enemies. The rumor that sea snakes (which live in the same oceans) eat these creatures is not true. Some sea snakes specialize in certain prey, such as fish eggs or eels; others eat a wide variety of fish. Most species are venomous.

Descendants of Australian land snakes, sea snakes are well adapted for marine life. They have flattened tails to help them swim. They can seal their mouths and nostrils to keep out water. Like all snakes, they have lungs, but sea snakes can also absorb oxygen directly from seawater through their skin. This is called *cutaneous respiration*, and it enables a sea snake to stay underwater for several hours before having to surface and breathe. Many of these species can be found in shallow water, but the highly venomous **yellow-bellied sea snake** (*Pelamis platurus*) is pelagic.

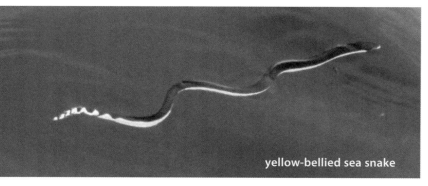
yellow-bellied sea snake

Another myth about sea snakes is that they have tiny fangs and can only penetrate the thin, tender skin between our fingers. The truth is that even though sea snakes have fixed fangs, these teeth are not especially tiny, and they can puncture human skin in many places on our bodies.

However, sea snakes are not usually inclined to bite people—and when they do bite, they often do not deliver venom. That's a good thing because their neuro- and *myotoxic* (affecting skeletal muscles) venom is quite potent.

An antivenin is available, and it can be used against all sea-snake envenomations, as well as that of **sea kraits** (*Laticauda*), which are also marine snakes. It's made from the venom of the **beaked sea snake** (*Enhydrina schistosa*), which is responsible for more than half of sea snake bites and ninety percent of fatalities caused by sea snakes. It isn't particularly aggressive, but it lives in shallow estuaries and more frequently comes into contact with people who fish and wade in these places, particularly in Southeast Asia.

It is unusual for a single species' antivenin to be effective against the bites of other species. The beaked sea snake's venom is a simple one, unlike the complex mixtures of toxins that make up land snakes' venoms. Dr. Bryan Fry believes that the simplicity of the venom comes from the simplicity of sea snakes' lives and diet: They eat fish and other small marine creatures, while land snakes eat a much wider variety of animals and live in more diverse habitats.

What *Isn't* This Fish Called?

a) turkeyfish
b) lionfish
c) dragonfish
d) zebrafish
e) butterfly cod
f) firefish
g) pajamafish

Believe it or not, it goes by every name except **g**. The gorgeous **lionfish** (*Pterois*), as it is most commonly called, is the cousin of the unattractive stonefish. Both are members of the venomous scorpionfish family. Like its camouflaged relatives, the aposematic maroon-striped lionfish has venomous spines in its fins, which it uses in self-defense. When it feels threatened, the fish opens its mouth wide and flares these fins. Males may also possibly use their spines to battle other males during mating season.

The lionfish is native to the Indo-Pacific area, where it is found swimming around reefs, often in shallow areas, and sometimes in bays, estuaries, and harbors. So, unless you take a trip to that area, you're not likely to encounter a lionfish, right? Not necessarily . . .

Lionfish are now found in the Atlantic Ocean from Florida to New York—and they are thriving, although mainly at depths of one hundred twenty feet or more, where the Gulf Stream warms the waters. How did they get there? The answer lies in the lionfish's looks. With their flashy stripes, lionfish have become popular aquarium fish in the U.S. In 1992, when Hurricane Andrew destroyed a Florida aquarium, six lionfish were accidentally released into Biscayne Bay. At other times, captive lionfish were probably set free on purpose by home-aquarium owners who didn't want to deal with toxic critters that grow large and eat the other fish in the tank. This practice of releasing animals in non-native areas is not only bad for the environment, but it's also against the law.

As lionfish thrive in the Atlantic, more people, such as divers and fishermen, are likely to encounter them—and therefore, to get stung. A lionfish's stab is usually not fatal, but it will cause severe pain and swelling, sometimes for days or weeks—even if the fish was not alive when the victim was stung. Dr. William Leo Smith found that out when he was a college student working in a pet shop that sold these fish. As he reached into a garbage pail into which a telephone had fallen, Smith got zapped by a dead lionfish that someone had thrown away.

Other venomous fish are also dangerous when deceased because the venom remains in the spines and is released by pressure. And sometimes the spines break and remain in a person's skin, causing infection. All in all, a goldfish or a guppy makes a much safer pet than a member of the scorpionfish clan.

Don't Tread on Me!

Many other toxic fishes are found in shallow waters. These benthic creatures are generally light brown or dark brown or speckled to blend with the mud, sand, rocks, or coral where they lie hidden. All have venomous spines on their backs or near their gills or both. Here are just a few varieties.

Toadfish (Batrachoididae)

There are forty-five species of **toadfish**, but not all are toxic. The venomous varieties are found in coastal Central and South America. Their toxins cause pain, swelling, dizziness, and fever, as well as wounds that take a long time to heal. One species, the **niquim** (*Thalassophryne nattereri*), is responsible for injuring many Brazilian fishermen yearly when they step on it or accidentally get jabbed by its spines as they try to remove it from a fishing net.

Why is it called a "toadfish"? Well, with its squat body and big mouth, it looks somewhat like a toad—and when it croaks or grunts, it sounds a bit like one, too.

Stargazer (*Uranoscopus*)

Found in coastal areas all around the world, this fish gets its name from—you guessed it—its eyes, which sit on top of its head, looking upward. Some species have a worm-shaped lure in their mouths. They wiggle it to attract their prey's attention, and then leap up to grab the victim. In addition to having venomous spines behind its gills, the **stargazer** can also deliver an electric shock to any enemy that dares to seize it.

Weever (*Trachinus*)

Weevers are found in the North Atlantic and the Mediterranean. When this fish lies buried in the sand, only the top of its head and the tips of its spines are visible. Its neurotoxic venom is painful, though not usually fatal. The treatment for its toxins (and that of many of the other venomous fishes) is soaking the affected limb in very hot water for thirty to ninety minutes and then repeating as often as necessary. The heat breaks down the protein in the venom.

Do Fish Like Venomous Worms?

Some do. Striped bass, king mackerel, whiting, and many other species love **bloodworms** (*Glycera dibranchiata*).

Bloodworms live in sandy, silty, or muddy shores. They are *polychaetes*—segmented marine worms with bristles called *setae*. Each worm can be more than a foot long, with a three-inch proboscis that is *eversible*—it can be turned inside out. The proboscis is tipped with four hard, venomous fangs for hunting and self-defense.

Most animals' teeth contain the mineral calcium. Scientists have recently discovered that bloodworm fangs are made of a combination of protein and copper. The bloodworm is the only species known to make its own copper teeth! Its bite can hurt for days, so wormers looking for bait have to be careful digging for and handling these critters.

Most **nemertines**, or **ribbon worms** (example: *Amphiporus bimaculatus*)—are benthic animals that live in shallow seas or coastal waters. They get their name from their great length. They are among the longest creatures in the sea. They're also called **proboscis worms** because they have an eversible proboscis they use to capture prey.

In some species the proboscis is equipped with a single thin stylet that injects neurotoxic venom. The stylet is usually released by the worm, or it breaks off upon striking the prey. When the worm withdraws its proboscis, it loads another stylet. A ribbon worm may have six stylets in reserve at any one time. Harmless to people, these worms hunt for small *invertebrates* (animals without backbones), such as other worms.

Another group of polychaetes, the **fireworms** (also called **bristleworms**), live on reefs, beneath stones, and in sea grass or mud (example: *Hermodice carunculata*). On their sides they have venomous setae that penetrate fish, then break off, releasing irritating venom. The venom doesn't kill the fish, but it may teach them to leave these worms alone. Any person pierced by a fireworm's setae will probably learn the same thing.

bloodworm

ribbon worm

fireworm

Danger Down Below

Sharks and big teeth go together. But sharks and venom? Yep. Just ask a **spiny dogfish** (*Squalus acanthias*).

A small shark that hunts in packs like canines, the spiny dogfish is something a fisherman doesn't care to snare. If this critter is caught in a fishing line, it will curl into a bow and strike with its two sharp spines. Each spine has a groove with a gland inside to make and pump venom. The bad news is that any fisherman pierced by these spines will be in pain for hours or even days. The good news is that he or she will survive.

There are several other venomous sharks. Some, like the spiny dogfish, can live in shallow

spiny dogfish

chimaera

or deep water—to depths of six hundred feet. A relative of the shark called the **chimaera** (example: *Chimaera monstrosa*) is almost never found above six hundred feet.

In Greek mythology, the chimaera is a monster with a lion's head, a goat's body, and a serpent's tail. The fishes of that name look monstrous and rather stitched together, too. Big-headed and big-eyed with a long, rat-like tail, the chimaera feeds on small animals that live near the bottom of the ocean. Unlike a shark, it has four large plates in its mouth instead of teeth. Because it dwells so deep in the water, few people have ever seen one—and fewer have probably been stabbed by its single spine.

A Meal to Remember—*If* You Live That Long

Some people have reported that chimaeras and many sharks are toxic to eat. However, the most dangerous food fish isn't a shark or a chimaera. It's the **puffer** (or **blowfish**). This fish gets its name from its ability to inflate itself so that it is too large for an enemy to swallow. Some species are prickly, as well. Not every species of puffer is poisonous, but many are. If a predator does manage to eat a toxic puffer, it will probably die because the fish's skin, blood, and organs contain tetrodotoxin, and each fish has enough of the stuff to kill thirty people or a dozen elephants. (Though the elephants are far less likely than humans to eat it!)

puffer fish

fugu

And humans *do* eat it—the tasty flesh and fins of one species, that is. In Japan, people order a variety of this expensive fish, known as **fugu** (*Fugu rubides*) in restaurants. Only special licensed chefs are allowed to prepare it. They have to remove the poisonous bits, and they must be very skilled because just a tiny amount of the fish's tetrodotoxin—enough to fit on a pinhead—can kill a person.

But the toxin may soon have a healing use, too. Scientists are now testing a drug made from it as a non-addictive painkiller for patients with cancer and other illnesses. In clinical trials, patients were treated with tiny amounts of the drug twice a day for four days. After three days, nearly seventy percent of them felt less pain. The relief often lasted way beyond the last injection—in some cases more than two weeks. Each fish can provide six hundred doses of the drug, so there is currently an ample supply. It will take more trials, but puffer poison may soon be a great new medicine on the market.

And Now for Something Completely Different...

They're cute, they're brilliantly colored, and they're toxic. Meet the **fanged blennies**, the only fish known to have venomous bites! The poison, used only in self-defense, flows up two fangs in the fish's lower jaw. The blenny can regulate its flow. Is this venom dangerous to humans? Not really. The blenny's bite has been compared to a wasp sting—nasty, but not deadly.

Some blennies have harmless imitators. The **golden mimic blenny** (*Plagiotremus laudanus flavus*) is a non-venomous fish that looks just like a **canary fang blenny** (*Meiacanthus oualanensis*). Predators avoid it, too.

Where are these unique fish found? Like some lionfish and stonefish, they live in the "rainforests of the oceans"— the coral reefs. And that's where we're headed next.

blenny

Caution! It's a Coral Reef

A ship is traveling through the darkness of outer space. The astronauts gazing at the earth below can see seas and mountains, but only one living thing. It's the vast Australian Great Barrier Reef, made up of coral.

Coral reefs are found not only in Australia, but also in warm, clear shallow ocean waters worldwide. They provide food and shelter for many sea creatures, they protect shorelines from erosion—and they produce lots and lots of venom.

Stony Stingers and Their Tenants

Many types of corals live in the world's oceans. All are *cnidarians* (ny-DAR-ee-ens). Cnidarians are among the oldest groups of animals. They have *tentacles*—feelers—covered with stinging darts called *nematocysts*. When an animal brushes against these nematocysts, they fire venom into its skin. Cnidarians use their venom to kill fish for food and to protect themselves.

Not all corals are reef builders. Only some species of **hard corals** (example: *Turbinaria*) have that ability. These corals form colonies that join together to construct organisms such as the Great Barrier Reef. A reef may look like bare rock, but it's made up of living animals and skeletons. Each hard coral on the reef creates a stony, calcium-carbonate outer case and hides inside it all day. Living corals build their cases on tops of the cases of dead ones. At night, the corals come out to feed, waving their tentacles and firing their nematocysts at tiny sea creatures that sweep by.

Most corals can't hurt people. But in Florida's waters and in the Caribbean, a relative of true corals called **fire coral** (*Millepora*) will make your skin burn if you touch it.

Fire coral got its name because if you touch it, you will feel a burn.

Plant or Animal? You Decide!

sundew   water lily   sea anemone   pitcher plant   sea urchin

Answer: The sea anemones and sea urchins are animals. Sundews and pitcher plants are carnivorous plants that feed on insects. The water lily is a lovely and non-carnivorous flower.

Flowers That Aren't

Reefs are rather like apartment houses, and a lot of their tenants are venomous. Venom is a powerful weapon for protection and hunting when there's so much competition for food and space. Many types of sea anemones live on reefs. These strange relatives of coral look like flowers, but they are animals—and they can sting.

Sea anemones can creep or float, but most of the time, they don't move. They are found in oceans all around the world, in both deep and shallow water, clinging to rocks, shells, coral, sand, and shipwrecks.

Each sea anemone is a cnidarian with a thick body topped by a mouth surrounded by a ring of fleshy, nematocyst-covered tentacles. Most species have nematocysts that are too weak to penetrate human skin, but some, such as the **branching anemone** (*Lebrunia danae*) and the **fire anemone** (*Actinodendron plumosum*), can sting people, and their venom causes itching, burning, swelling, and severe pain.

sea anemone

Hydra-Phobia

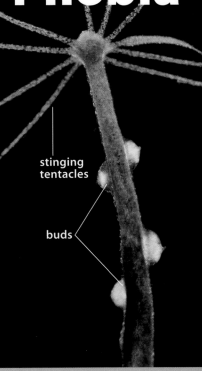

stinging tentacles

buds

The **hydra** (*Hydra*) is a small, freshwater relative of the sea anemone—another cnidarian with stinging tentacles. It eats tiny critters such as water fleas and insect larvae and is no danger to large animals.

In Greek mythology, the Hydra was a many-headed monster. If you cut off one head, two would grow in its place. Though our little hydra friend can reproduce through the mating of a male and female, it can also do so by budding, with no male required, just as corals can. Budded baby hydras just grow right out of their mother's "sides." A hydra can have as many as four buds, which turn into offspring—and no beheading is required!

Finding Nemo

clownfish

A few animals eat sea anemones. Many others avoid them. But not the anemonefishes, such as this **clownfish** (*Amphiprion ocellaris*) made famous in the animated film *Finding Nemo*.

Clownfishes and their relatives live in the anemones, feeding on algae and plankton. These fish have a thick coating of mucus that makes them immune to the anemones' stings. Some anemonefish have a specific type of anemone as their partner. Others visit several varieties of anemones. The fish are protected by the cnidarians, and, though no one is sure what the anemones get in return, it is possible that the fish protect them by chasing away predators.

There are two current theories about how and where the anemonefish gets its mucus covering.

One is "acclimatization"—the fish swims for hours among the anemone's tentacles, making brief contact, receiving non-lethal stings, and smearing the mucus from the cnidarian onto its own body. A second theory states that the mucus comes from the fish, and it lacks an element that causes the anemone to fire its nematocysts.

Both theories may be true. For anemonefish that visit several species of anemones, the acclimatization theory makes sense. For anemonefish that have just one host, the mucus theory may be more relevant.

I Have an Anemone, and I Know How to Use It!

Another critter that doesn't fear sea anemones is the **hermit crab**. Unlike other crabs, hermits don't have their own shell-like coverings. They slip into the abandoned shells of mollusks—soft-bodied, shell-making animals—such as snails and whelks. Several types of hermit crabs gather sea anemones and stick them to their shells for protection. The anemones may benefit by getting leftover scraps of the crabs' food. A single crab may wear as many as six anemones on its shell.

Another species, the **boxer crab** (*Lybia tessellata*) of Australia, holds anemones in each of its claws and, like boxing gloves, thrusts them at enemies. It may also use the anemones to stun prey.

hermit crab with anemones on shell

boxer crab holding anemones

Flowers with Jaws

They're round. They're colorful. They're the pincushions of the sea. They're the sea urchins, and you'll find them feeding mostly on algae on reefs, in tide pools, sandy shallows, and rocky rubble, as well as in deep water on sea beds.

Sea urchins are *echinoderms*—animals known for *radial symmetry* (arms or rays arranged in a pattern around a central body) and tube feet that move through a pumping action. Most, but not all, echinoderms have spiny skins. Sea urchins' spines, used for protection, can be short or long, depending on the species. They can break off in your skin and cause infection. Some urchins, such as the **fire urchin** (*Asthenosoma varium*) have venomous spines, which cause more serious pain and swelling, and sometimes numbness, irregular heartbeat, and other symptoms.

Besides their spines, urchins, as well as sea stars, have *pedicellariae*—tiny pincers on stalks used for self-defense and cleaning. In the **flower sea urchin** (*Toxopneustes pileolus*), these pedicellariae make the creature appear to be a big blossom. But anyone who touches these "petals" is in for a nasty surprise. Within them are venomous jaws that deliver a painful bite, as well as possible paralysis and respiratory distress. These pincers can hang on and keep pumping venom even if they're pulled out of the urchin's body, so they have to be removed from a victim as quickly as possible. Heat helps break down the venom. On the Seychelles Islands in the Indian Ocean, people bitten by these urchins sometimes put hot oil or drip candle wax onto the punctures to stop the pain.

flower sea urchin

The Venomous Star of the Sea

Sea stars are the urchins' cousins. There are eighteen hundred species of this echinoderm—but only one is known to be venomous: the Australian **crown-of-thorns starfish** (*Acanthaster planci*). Its spines, used for self-defense, can cause painful wounds and even paralyze a person.

But the crown-of-thorns is more deadly to coral—and for that it doesn't use its spines. It uses its stomach, which it pushes out through its mouth. Strong acids dissolve the coral polyps, and small hairs collect the gooey food and carry it inside the sea star. Adult crown-of-thorns sea stars eat only coral, and large numbers of them can destroy entire reefs. Population explosions of these echinoderms regularly occur, and experts have many theories as to what causes the outbreaks, from natural occurrences to human impact. The good thing is that through studying this animal, people are learning a lot about the ecosystem of the reefs.

crown-of-thorns starfish

Vegetables
That Aren't

The reefs are home to many other echinoderms. Spineless **sea cucumbers** (example: *Holothuria leucospilota*), with their long bodies and tough skin, look like . . . cucumbers. Also found in other habitats such as bedrock, sand, and eelgrass beds, and in waters both shallow and deep, sea cucumbers can expel their organs if they're startled by preda-

sea cucumber

tors—and then regrow them. Some sea cucumbers will first produce sticky threads in self-defense. These contain a neurotoxin called *holothurin*, which is deadly to fish and small mammals.

Believe it or not, sea cucumbers—including their spewed intestines—are eaten in many Asian countries and elsewhere. They have to be carefully cleaned, a process that takes days.

Sea cucumbers spew their insides when they are surprised.

They are also prized for medicinal properties. The flesh and mucus may lower blood pressure, reduce inflammation, heal wounds, and even slow aging. Because of the high demand for these delicacies, sea cucumbers are being over-harvested and even illegally harvested in some parts of the world. Numerous organizations are currently trying to address this serious problem.

Sponges to Stay Away From

Many types of **sponges** (*Porifera*) also live on the reefs. Poriferans don't have mouths. Instead, they have tiny pores to draw in water. Cells in their body walls filter plankton and other food from the water as it's pumped in and then out of the sponge's body through larger openings.

Sponges come in all shapes and sizes. Some look like big holey cheeses or fingers or chimneys, while others resemble vases, bushes, or flat sheets. None are venomous—they can't bite or sting—but a few, such as the **fire** and **touch-me-not sponges** (*Tedania ignis* and *Neofibularia nolitangere*) are

poisonous if handled. They have toxins that can cause rashes and swelling.

Fire sponges have red or orange warning colors to announce that they're toxic. But the most venomous sea creature in the world can switch from warning coloration to camouflage and back again with ease. And it has four times as many arms as you do!

fire sponge

Eight Arms to Hold You

blue-ringed octopus

Found on reefs and in tide pools, caves, holes, and submerged old bottles and cans, the **blue-ringed octopus** (*Hapalochlaena*) of coastal Australia starts life the size of a pea and grows to the size of a golf ball. When it is hunting or hiding, its camouflage colors are light yellow to dark brown, but when it is threatened, its aposematic colors are bright yellow with electric-blue rings. If this creature bites you with its parrot-like beak, those colors may be the last ones you'll ever see.

All octopuses probably use toxic saliva to kill prey such as crabs, but none of them are deadly to people except for the blue-ringed species. It is not an aggressive animal at all, but it will bite enemies that provoke it. Because the mollusk (its shell is inside instead of outside) is so little and cute, people sometimes pick it up—and that's how they get bitten. Its beak can pierce a diver's wetsuit.

The bite is painless, but the octopus delivers saliva that contains highly dangerous tetradotoxin.

Within minutes, the victim is paralyzed. Soon, he or she can no longer breathe. There is no antivenin. The only way to save the victim is by giving mouth-to-mouth resuscitation (rescue breathing) and heart massage for hours until the person begins to breathe again on his or her own. If the victim lives through the first twenty-four hours after being bitten, he or she usually will recover completely.

The blue-ringed octopus adult is only as large as a golf ball.

One Tongue to Kill You

People have long appreciated the beauty of mollusks. Some collect their shells. That's a fine hobby, as long as the animals aren't endangered species—and as long as the collector doesn't get zapped by a live and deadly **cone shell** (also called **cone snail**).

striated cone shell

Many mollusks have a long tongue called a *radula* that is covered with small, hard teeth used for drilling into or rasping away at food. But the venomous cone shells' teeth are different—they can inject *conotoxin*, which paralyzes and kills prey. Each tooth is a harpoon that sends out a fine thread to hook a fish, worm, or another mollusk. Then the cone shell pulls in its catch.

This allows the slow-moving mollusk to capture faster prey. Sometimes the catch is human.

Like other venomous animals, cone shells aren't interested in humans as food. However, in self-defense a shell will harpoon folks who pick it up. Those folks are often collectors drawn to the shell's beautiful colors and its elegant shape. Like the blue-ringed octopus's beak, the cone shell's harpoon can pierce a wetsuit or gloves, and, depending on the species, its nearly painless sting can be fatal. There is no

the radula of a cone shell

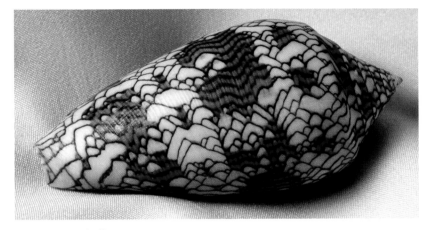
textile cone shell

antivenin, and victims may require mouth-to-mouth resuscitation and heart massage. There have been about thirty reported cone shell deaths since 1935—and perhaps others that were unrecorded.

Among the most dangerous species found on reefs, sand, and rubble in the warm, shallow waters of the Indo-Pacific are the **striated cone** (*Conus striatus*), the **tulip cone** (*Conus tulipa*), the **textile cone** (*Conus textile*), and the **geographic cone** (*Conus geographus*). These mollusks produce different toxins at different times, probably to suit different prey. A cone shell might never use the exact same combination of toxins twice! Scientists are studying these toxins for medical uses, especially as non-addictive painkillers. One is already on the market.

Besides their potential for medical use, cone shells also provide food for people in places such as the Philippines and Samoa. The venom isn't toxic when eaten. How do hunters gather these shells? VERY CAREFULLY!

Cone shells' colors are good camouflage against rocks, coral, and sand. They blend in well, making them hard for their victims to spot. Another group of venomous sea creatures is also hard to see because they're see-through. But you can see them on the next page.

Polyp or Medusa?

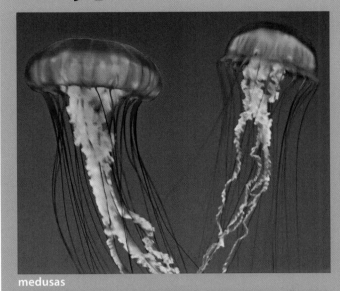
medusas

polyps

Corals are not the only cnidarians. This large group also includes sea anemones, jellyfish, hydras, Portuguese man-of-wars, and other creatures. Their bodies are basically a sac with a single opening for feeding and waste evacuation, and all of them can sting.

Cnidarians have two main forms: **polyps** and **medusas**. Polyps are tube-like with mouths that face upward. They affix themselves to rocks, plants, and other bases and hardly move. Medusas are round and free-swimming with mouths that point downward.

Sailing, Sailing, Over the TOXIC Main!

Water, water, everywhere, and not a drop to drink? Too true, if you're traveling the earth's oceans. Oceans are salty bodies of water that cover more than seventy percent of our planet. They're divided into numerous zones from the photic (where sunlight can reach) to the trenches, the deepest of which is nearly thirty-six thousand feet.

People have been sailing these waters for many millennia. But jellyfish have been traveling them for millions of years.

A Toast to Jellies

Most of these blobs cannot kill people; however, a few are lethal. We call them all **jellyfish**, but they aren't fish at all. They're *cnidarians*. Remember that these animals can be polyps *or* medusas. Well, most jellyfish are both.

They start life as small larvae called *planula*. Then they attach themselves to a surface and become polyps. These divide and bud into *ephyra*—free-swimming youngsters that change into little medusas. The medusas grow into the full-sized adults we see in oceans and aquariums.

Found at all ocean depths (and some even in freshwater), jellyfish are about ninety-five percent water. They have no backbones, brains, noses, or ears, but they can detect light and odors through their nervous system. They swim by pumping their umbrella-like bells, also called floats. This pumping action lets jellyfish move vertically. But to move any great distance horizontally, they must rely on ocean currents, tides, and winds.

jellyfish

Underneath their bells are leaf-like "arms" to bring food to their mouths and thread-like tentacles covered with nematocysts, which fire neurotoxic venom into prey or predators that brush against them. A single tentacle can have hundreds or thousands of nematocysts that fire in micro-seconds—even if the tentacle breaks off or the jellyfish is dead. So when folks tell you not to touch a jellyfish on the sand, they're not kidding!

Man, That's Some Man-of-War!

The **Portuguese man-of-war** (*Physalia physalis*), also called a "bluebottle," is not a jellyfish. Related to the tiny hydra, it is actually a group of different types of polyps attached together beneath an air-filled float. It is carried along on the water's surface by the waves and ocean currents.

The Portuguese man-of-war's tentacles can extend sixty-five feet below its purple-blue float. They can inflict stings that feel like electrical shocks and cause joint and muscle pain, faintness, nausea, chills, and fever, but they are usually not lethal.

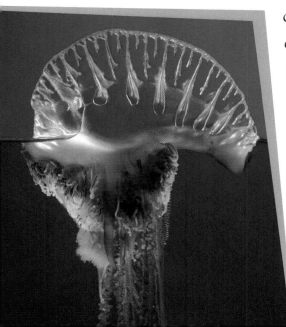

Portuguese man-of-war

Deadly or Not?

Which of these jellyfish could be *deadly?*

1 moon jelly

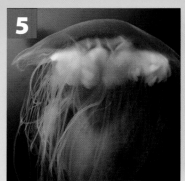
2 barrel jelly

3 comb jelly

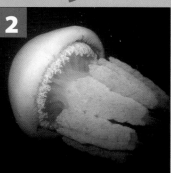
4 sea wasp

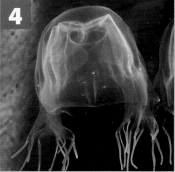
5 lion's mane

6 Irukandji jelly

Answers: **4, 5,** and **6** are dangerous jellies; **1, 2,** and **3** are not. In fact, comb jellies are not actually jellyfish. They are relatives that do not sting; they catch small prey with a sticky substance on their tentacles.

Jellyfish? No Problem!

Most fish avoid jellyfish. But some, such as the **whiting** (*Merlangius merlangus*) and the **man-of-war fish** (*Nomeus gronovii*) do just the opposite. The whiting's host is the enormous lion's mane jellyfish, which can be as wide as eight feet with tentacles up to one hundred twenty feet long.

lion's mane jellyfish and whiting

man-of-war fish with Portuguese man-of-war

When a whiting is threatened, it hides under the jellyfish for protection. The man-of-war fish lives with the Portuguese man-of-war, feeding on its tentacles, which then regrow. How does the fish do this? It appears to be immune to jellyfish venom. It may have a special coating on its body that keeps the nematocysts from stinging.

Other animals, such as the **leatherback turtle** (*Dermochelys coriacea*), can also eat jellyfish tentacles without getting poisoned. Unfortunately, turtles are harmed by eating plastic bags that they mistake for jellyfish—one good reason for people to recycle these items, to prevent illegal dumping of garbage in the ocean, and to come up with better ways of managing waste disposal.

Some **nudibranches** or **sea slugs** (*Glaucus atlanticus* and *Glaucilla marginata*) can feast on the Portuguese man-of-war without triggering the nematocysts to fire. The darts get stored inside the nudibranch's body, so when a fish tries to eat the sea slug, the fish gets stung.

leatherback turtle

sea slugs

Jellyfish? Problem!

People and other animals don't have a whiting's or a nudibranch's protection. A jellyfish or Portuguese man-of-war's nematocysts can sting us through thin clothes or rubber gloves. Most stings can cause blisters, a rash, and pain. The lion's mane has a sting that can kill. It is featured as the innocent murderer in a famous Sherlock Holmes story, "The Adventure of the Lion's Mane". This jellyfish's size and the strength of its venom are what make it dangerous.

The **sea nettle** (*Chrysaora*) is another large jellyfish that packs a nasty, though not usually deadly, sting. Some species, such as the **black sea nettle** (*Chrysaora achlyos*), can be more than three feet wide with twenty-five-foot-long tentacles. In 1989, huge numbers of black sea nettles appeared off the coast of San Diego, California. They mysteriously vanished. Then, ten years later, they bloomed—reappeared in record numbers.

Scientists think the reappearance may be due to more food for these cnidarians caused by increased nutrients from agricultural run-off and other human activity.

But size doesn't always matter. The box jellyfish family, which includes the **sea wasps** and the **Irukandji jellyfish** of the Indo-Pacific, are smaller than the lion's mane, but they are the most deadly cnidarians of all. Unlike other jellyfish, the peanut-sized Irukandji with four three-foot-long tentacles, produces a sting that feels mild at first. But after about thirty minutes or so, it causes a severe reaction called "Irukandji syndrome," a condition of severe muscle spasms, a burning sensation, and back and kidney pain that can last for hours or days.

sea nettles

Dr. Jamie Seymour of James Cook University in Cairns, Australia, and an Irukandji jellyfish

Sea wasps can reach the size of a basketball with tentacles more than ten feet long. Their venom can be fatal to people in as few as three minutes, causing heart or respiratory failure. In fact, one species, *Chironex fleckeri*, has been called the most venomous marine animal in the world. It has caused many injuries and more than sixty recorded deaths. So far, there is no antivenin.

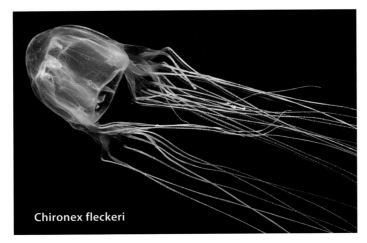

Chironex fleckeri

In Australia, swimmers once commonly used pantyhose to avoid being stung by these dangerous critters. A sea wasp's nematocysts are short. They can't pierce two layers of nylon. Now special stinger suits made of Lycra® are available. But they don't protect a swimmer or diver's face, hands, or feet. Recently, a team of marine biologists developed a sunscreen with a repellent that fools the jellyfish into thinking the person is neither predator nor prey. They tested it on themselves and didn't get stung once. It could certainly be a promising product for folks who like to swim in dangerous waters.

If You Get Stung by a Jellyfish or Its Cousin

Don't panic! Thrashing around will only make it fire more nematocysts. If you're in the water, call for a lifeguard. Get medical help as soon as you can. Ask someone to help you carefully scrape off any clinging tentacles by first applying shaving cream or a paste of baking soda or mud and then shaving the area with a razor, a credit card, a key, or something else with an edge.

As far as home remedies go, here are the ones that work: white vinegar, meat tenderizer, baking soda, or salt water applied to your skin. Ones that don't work include: ice, fresh water, ammonia, alcohol, or urine. Those liquids will cause more nematocysts to fire (and the last one might embarrass you, too).

Jelly with Toast (or Maybe Rice)

Jellyfish are food not only for fish, turtles, and other marine creatures, but also for people. Marinated jellyfish is a popular appetizer in Chinese and other Asian cuisines. What does this rubbery dish taste like? Not like fish or chicken or anything meaty. More like a pickled vegetable. How does this author know? She's eaten it!

Conclusion:
Let's Hear It for the Toxic!

One summer day in 2006, I went to the American Museum of Natural History's exhibit, "Lizards and Snakes: Alive!" I got to see a black mamba, a Gaboon viper, a red spitting cobra, a Gila monster, and other reptiles up close. The exhibit was entertaining and educational—and so were the people attending it. Some were fascinated. Others had the creeps. Still others were fascinated *and* had the creeps.

Whenever we encounter animals that can hurt us, we have strong reactions. And we should. It makes sense to be both curious about and wary of dangerous creatures, whether they are reptiles, amphibians, insects, spiders, mammals, fish, birds, cnidarians, or something else.

But it also makes sense to protect these creatures. Why? For one thing, because they do so much good. Some pollinate plants so that we can have fruits, flowers, vegetables and other crops. Others eat pests that destroy these crops or vermin that spread diseases. Some venomous animals themselves are edible. From others, we get medicines. And think of how many have inspired poems, stories, paintings, films, and other works of art!

But venomous and poisonous animals also deserve our respect simply because they're alive, and they deserve to stay that way.

Unfortunately, many of these animals are in danger. They are losing their habitats or are being sickened by pollutants and waste. They are being sold as pets—or killed by pets. They are slaughtered by people for their skins, for souvenirs, or simply for no better reason than because folks just don't like them.

Unless we learn to appreciate these creatures, we won't safeguard them and their environments. If we don't safeguard them, we will never uncover or understand all the marvels of venom and other biotoxins. We will lose the grace of a jellyfish, the trill of a toad, the beauty of a butterfly, the surprise of a snake, and even the awesome scariness of a big, hairy spider with its venomous fangs—and that would be a big loss indeed.

tarantula

Acknowledgments

Many thanks to my husband, Steve Aronson; his brother, Dr. Bill Aronson; my editor, Tanya Dean, and the crew of Darby Creek Publishing; Mary Cash of Holiday House who initiated this book, and to the following wonderful experts:

Dr. Barbara Brown, American Museum of Natural History, www.amnh.org

David Dickey, American Museum of Natural History

Dr. Bryan Grieg Fry, Melbourne University, www.venomdoc.com

Chris Harper, Southeastern Hot Herp Society, www.venomousreptiles.org

Ray Hunter, www.cobraman.net

Graham Milledge, Australian Museum, www.amonline.net.au

Lee Moore, www.serpentoxin.com

Peter Rees, www.traveldoctor.co.uk/index.htm

Vimoksalehi Lukoschek, James Cook University, http://homes.jcu.edu.au/~sci-bhl

A special thanks to my fabulous fact checkers:

Bill Holmstrom, Bronx Zoo of the Wildlife Conservation Society, www.bronxzoo.com

Paul Sieswerda, New York Aquarium of the WCS, www.nyaquarium.com

Louis Sorkin, American Museum of Natural History

Bibliography

I read many books for research. Here are some of them:

Aaseng, Nathan, *Poisonous Creatures*, Brookfield, CT: Twenty-First Century Books, 1997.

Allen, Gerald, *Marine Life of the Pacific and Indian Oceans*, Clarendon, VT: Periplus Books, 2000.

Attenborough, David, *Life in the Undergrowth*, Princeton, NJ: Princeton University Press, 2005.

Eisner, Thomas, *For Love of Insects*, Cambridge, MA: Belknap Press, 2003.

Eisner, Thomas, Maria Eisner, and Melody Siegler, *Secret Weapons: Defenses of Insects, Spiders, Scorpions, and Other Many-Legged Creatures*, Cambridge, MA: Belknap Press, 2005.

Ernst, Carl H. and George R. Zug, *Snakes in Question*, Washington, DC: Smithsonian Institution Press, 1996.

Foster, Steven and Roger Caras, *A Field Guide to Venomous Animals and Poisonous Plants*, Boston: Houghton-Mifflin Co., 1994.

Freiberg, Dr. Marcos and Jerry G. Walls, *The World of Venomous Animals*, Neptune City, NJ: T.F.H. Publications, 1984.

Landau, Matthew, *Poisonous, Venomous, and Electric Marine Organisms of the Atlantic Coast, Gulf of Mexico, and the Caribbean*, Medford, NJ: Plexus Publishing, 1997.

Mattison, Chris, *Encyclopedia of North American Reptiles and Amphibians*, San Diego, CA: Thunder Bay Press, 2005.

O'Shea, Mark, *Venomous Snakes of the World*, Princeton, NJ: Princeton University Press, 2005.

O'Toole, Christopher, *Alien Empire*, New York: HarperCollins Publishers, 1995.

Preston-Mafham, Rod and Ken, *Encyclopedia of Insects and Spiders*, San Diego, CA: Thunder Bay Press, 2005.

Waldbauer, Dr. Gilbert, *The Handy Bug Answer Book*, Detroit: Visible Ink Press, 1998.

Waldbauer, Gilbert, *Insects Through the Seasons*, Cambridge, MA: Harvard University Press, 1996.

Waldbauer, Gilbert, *Millions of Monarchs, Bunches of Beetles*, Cambridge, MA: Harvard University Press, 2000.

Waller, Geoffrey, editor, *SeaLife: A Complete Guide to the Marine Environment*, Washington, D.C.: Smithsonian Institution Press, 1996.

Webliography

I spent a lot of time on the Internet, too. These are some of the best sites and articles, listed in the same order as this book:

General, all animals

http://animaldiversity.ummz.umich.edu/site/index.html
http://tolweb.org/tree/phylogeny.html
http://amnh.org

General, toxic animals

http://library.thinkquest.org/C007974/2animal.htm
http://www.afpmb.org/pubs/Field_Guide/field_guide.htm
http://pubs.acs.org/cen/critter/critterchemistry.html

General, venom cure

http://www.pbs.org/wnet/nature/venomcure/index.html
Dr. Bryan Fry's site: http://venomdoc.com

Australian animals

http://www.amonline.net.au/research/index.cfm
http://www.barrierreefaustralia.com
http://www.reptilepark.com.au/default.asp
http://www.sydneyaquarium.com.au/Spotlights/SPO010.asp
http://www.pbs.org/wnet/nature/australia/land.html

American desert animals

http://www.desertusa.com/index.html

General, insects

http://www.insecta-inspecta.com
http://bugguide.net/node/view/15740

Spiders and insects

http://insects.tamu.edu/extension/bulletins/l-1787.html
http://spiders.ucr.edu/dermatol.html
http://www.entomology.ucr.edu/ebeling/ebel9-1.html

Tarantulas

http://www.nationalgeographic.com/tarantulas/index2.html

Black widows

http://ohioline.osu.edu/hyg-fact/2000/2061A.html

Brown recluses

http://spiders.ucr.edu/recluseid.html

Sydney funnel-webs

http://www.faunanet.gov.au/wos/factfile.cfm?Fact_ID=84

Ticks

http://www.idph.state.il.us/envhealth/pccommonticks.htm
http://medent.usyd.edu.au/photos/tick_photos.htm

Centipedes

http://www.earthlife.net/insects/chilopod.html
http://www.uky.edu/Ag/CritterFiles/casefile/relatives/centipedes/centipede.htm

Millipedes

http://www.earthlife.net/insects/diplopoda.html
http://www.ipm.iastate.edu/ipm/iiin/mmilliped.html

Bees

http://www.gpnc.org/honeybee.htm
http://www.thebigzoo.com/Animals/Honey_Bee.asp
http://www.bumblebee.org
http://www.everythingabout.net/articles/biology/animals/arthropods/insects/
    bees/carpenter_bee/index.shtml
http://www.si.edu/resource/faq/nmnh/buginfo/killbee.htm
http://www.discover.com/issues/jun-03/features/featstung

Wasps

http://www.everythingabout.net/articles/biology/animals/arthropods/insects/
    wasps/index.shtml
http://www.bbc.co.uk/nature/wildfacts/factfiles/427.shtml
http://ohioline.osu.edu/hyg-fact/2000/2078.html
http://news.nationalgeographic.com/news/2005/08/0817_050817_
    waspsaliva.html
http://insects.tamu.edu/fieldguide/cimg344.html

Ladybugs

http://home.att.net/~larvalbugbio/ladybug.html
http://www.nysaes.cornell.edu/ent/biocontrol/predators/c7.html

Monarch butterflies

http://www.monarchwatch.org
http://www.insecta-inspecta.com/butterflies/monarch/index.html

Fireflies

http://iris.biosci.ohio-state.edu/projects/FFiles
http://www.news.cornell.edu/Chronicle/97/9.4.97/firefly.html

Rattlebox moths

http://www.news.cornell.edu/releases/May99/ornatrix_tricks.hrs.html

Stinging caterpillars

http://www.uky.edu/Ag/Entomology/entfacts/misc/ef003.htm
http://cals.arizona.edu/urbanipm/insects/stingingcaterpillars.html

Blister beetles

http://www.uky.edu/Ag/Entomology/entfacts/fldcrops/ef102.htm

Assassin bug

http://www.uky.edu/Ag/CritterFiles/casefile/insects/bugs/assassin/assassin.htm

Mosquitoes

http://science.howstuffworks.com/mosquito.htm

Ants

http://edis.ifas.ufl.edu/IG080
http://www.tightloop.com/ants/index.php
http://www.myrmecos.net/index.html
http://uts.cc.utexas.edu/~gilbert/research/fireants/faq.html
http://www.infiniteworld.org/research/introduction.htm
http://news.nationalgeographic.com/news/2005/09/0921_050921_
    amazon_ant.html

Webliography

General, reptiles, amphibians

http://www.herpnet.net/Iowa-Herpetology/index.html
http://www.californiaherps.com/index.html
http://www.livingunderworld.org/amphibianArticles/article0011.shtml

Snakes

http://www.venomousreptiles.org
http://www.discoverychannel.ca/animals/snakeshome
http://www.pbs.org/wnet/nature/reptiles/snakes.html
http://www.szgdocent.org/resource/rr/c-kill.htm
http://www.flmnh.ufl.edu/natsci/herpetology/fl-guide/venomsnk.htm
http://www.texas-venomous.com/speciesindex.html
http://www.nationalparks.nsw.gov.au/npws.nsf/Content/Snakes
http://serpentoxin.com/index.html
http://news.nationalgeographic.com/news/2001/10/1004_snakefears.html

Sea snakes

http://homes.jcu.edu.au/~sci-bhl

Frogs and toads

http://www.sandiegozoo.org/animalbytes/t-frog_toad.html
http://www.fdrproject.org/pages/toads.htm

Poison Dart Frogs

http://www.amnh.org/exhibitions/frogs
http://www.tigerhomes.org/animal/poison-dart-frogs.cfm

Salamanders and newts

http://www.sandiegozoo.org/animalbytes/t-salamander.html
http://www.caudata.org

Shrews

http://www.inhs.uiuc.edu/inhsreports/jan-feb99/shrew.html

Platypuses

http://www.epa.qld.gov.au/nature_conservation/wildlife/native_
    animals/platypus

Birds

http://nationalzoo.si.edu/Publications/ZooGoer/2001/2/
    intoxnewguineabirds.cfm
http://news.nationalgeographic.com/news/2004/11/1109_
    041109_toxic_beetles.html

Lizards

http://www.newscientist.com/article.ns?id=dn8331

Scorpions

http://www.ub.ntnu.no/scorpion-files/index.php
http://www.museums.org.za/bio/scorpions/index.htm

General, marine animals

http://www.mbayaq.org/default.asp
http://umed.med.utah.edu/get_involved/clubs/international/
    presentations/dangers.html
http://www.edge-of-reef.com/inggris/laben.htm
http://striweb.si.edu/bocas_database/phylums.php?kingdom=Animal

General, fish

http://www.amnh.org/science/papers/venomous_fish.php
http://www.flmnh.ufl.edu/fish

Catfish

http://silurus.acnatsci.org

Stingrays

http://www.mote.org/index.php?src=gendocs&link=Stingrays&category=
    Shark%20Research&submenu=INFO

Lionfish

http://www.stlzoo.org/animals/abouttheanimals/fish/lionfish.htm
http://www.oceanservice.noaa.gov/education/stories/lionfish/lion05_stop.html

Pufferfish

http://www.abc.net.au/science/news/stories/s1000732.htm

Blennies

http://www.wetwebmedia.com/sabertoothblens.htm

Ribbon worms

http://www.reefkeeping.com/issues/2004-01/rs/index.php
http://www.ucmp.berkeley.edu/nemertini/nemertini.html

Fireworms (Bristleworms)

http://scilib.ucsd.edu/sio/nsf/fguide/annelida.html

General, cnidarians

http://www.ucihs.uci.edu/biochem/steele/default.html
http://tolweb.org/tree?group=Cnidaria&contgroup=Animals

Corals and Reefs

http://www.coralreefalliance.org/index.php?option=com_content&
    task=section&id=1&Itemid=3
http://www.uvi.edu/coral.reefer
http://www.gbrmpa.gov.au

Sea anemones

http://www.wetwebmedia.com/marine/inverts/cnidaria/anthozoa/
    twaanemones.htm

Echinoderms

http://www.ucmp.berkeley.edu/echinodermata/echinodermata.html

Sponges

http://www.ucmp.berkeley.edu/porifera/porifera.html

Cone shells

http://grimwade.biochem.unimelb.edu.au/cone/index1.html

Jellyfish

http://jellieszone.com
http://www.dnr.sc.gov/marine/pub/seascience/jellyfi.html
http://www.nationalgeographic.com/ngkids/9608/jellyfish
http://www.aquarium.org/jellies
http://www.jcu.edu.au/interest/stingers/index.htm
http://www.ucmp.berkeley.edu/cnidaria/cubozoa.html

Portuguese man-of-wars

http://www.austmus.gov.au/factsheets/bluebottle.htm

Sea slugs

http://www.seaslugforum.net

Glossary

aculeus: the stinger of a scorpion, bee, ant, or wasp.

alarm pheromone: a chemical signal given off by animals, especially insects, that alerts members of their group to danger.

amphibian: a cold-blooded animal with a backbone that is generally born in a moist place. It breathes first through gills, then later through lungs. Amphibians include frogs, toads, and salamanders.

anaphylactic shock: a severe systemic allergic reaction that can lead to death.

anthropophobia: fear of people or society.

antibodies: proteins used by the body's immune system to identify and destroy germs, viruses, and toxins.

anticoagulant: a substance that prevents blood from clotting.

anting: behavior by birds in which they rub or allow ants on their feathers, possibly to stimulate the insects to spray formic acid.

antivenin: serum given to victims to treat the effects of venom. Also called *antivenom*.

apiary: a place where beehives are kept, usually to raise bees for honey.

apitherapy: the use of bee products to treat diseases and other conditions and to promote good health.

aposematic: using warning colors and patterns by animals to announce that they taste bad and may be toxic. Noun form: *aposematism*.

aquatic: living in the water; *semi-aquatic*: living partly on land and partly in the water.

arachnid: an animal with eight jointed legs, two main body sections, and a hard, outer covering, or *exoskeleton*. Arachnids include spiders, ticks, and scorpions.

arboreal: living in trees or bushes.

barbels: whisker-like organs near the mouths of some fishes used to help find food.

batrachotoxin: a cardio- and neurotoxin found in some poisonous birds and frogs.

benthic: living on the bottom of oceans, lakes, rivers, and other bodies of water.

beta blockers: drugs used to treat cardiovascular diseases.

biotoxin: a toxin from an animal or plant.

budding: a form of reproduction in which the offspring grows out of the body of its parent. Corals, hydras, and other animals can reproduce by budding.

camouflage: the use of colors and patterns by animals to disguise themselves from predators and prey.

cantharidin: a poisonous chemical substance secreted by many species of blister beetles.

cardiotoxin: a toxin that destroys the heart and blood vessels.

carrion: dead flesh.

cartilage: connective tissue found in many animals. The skeletons of sharks and rays are made of cartilage instead of bone.

chelicerae: the pointed mouthparts of spiders and other animals used to grasp food. A spider's fangs are at the ends of its chelicerae.

cnidarian: an animal, usually aquatic, with radial symmetry, stinging cells in its tentacles, and no backbone. Cnidarians include corals, sea anemones, and jellyfish.

cold-blooded: taking on the temperature of its surroundings. *Cold-blooded* animals, such as reptiles and amphibians, use sunlight/heat to warm up and then retreat into the shade so they don't get too hot. *Warm-blooded* animals, including birds and mammals, have a constant body temperature, regardless of the outside heat or cold.

conotoxin: a neurotoxin produced by cone shells.

constriction: the method used by some snakes to kill prey by wrapping around and squeezing the victim.

contortrostatin: a protein isolated in copperhead venom that shows promise in stopping the growth of certain cancerous growths.

cutaneous respiration: the ability of amphibians and other animals to take in oxygen through moist skin.

drone: a male bee. Drones are stingless.

echinoderm: an aquatic animal with tube feet, radial symmetry, and spiny or tough skin. Sea stars, sea urchins, and sea cucumbers are echinoderms.

entomologist: a scientist who studies insects.

envenomation: the injection of venom into a victim.

enzymes: protein molecules that speed up chemical reactions in the body.

ephyra: a young, free-swimming jellyfish that has budded from a polyp and will change into the adult stage, or *medusa*.

epinephrine: a hormone produced by the adrenal glands located above the kidneys. If stung, people with a severe allergy to bee venom may need a shot of epinephrine to survive.

estuary: an area where freshwater and seawater mix.

eversible: able to turn inside out.

fangs: sharp, pointed teeth that are grooved or hollow in venomous animals.

formic acid: a toxic substance sprayed by some species of ants for attack and defense.

hemotoxin: a toxin that destroys red blood cells, disrupts blood clotting, and causes organ and tissue damage.

holothurin: a neurotoxin produced by some sea cucumbers.

hormone: a chemical messenger that gives instructions to various parts of the body.

ichthyologist: a scientist who studies fish.

immune: having resistance to disease or toxins.

insect: an animal with six jointed legs, three body segments, and a hard, outer covering, or *exoskeleton*.

invertebrate: an animal, such as an insect, spider, or worm, without a backbone. A *vertebrate* is an animal with a backbone.

larva: a young animal that will *metamorphose*, or change into an adult that is different in appearance. Plural: *larvae*

localized reaction: a response to toxins or other substances that takes place right around the site of a sting, bite, or source of the irritation.

lucibufagins: toxic self-defense chemicals found in some species of fireflies.

lymphatic system: a system that circulates *lymph*, a fluid that protects the body from infection and other disorders. When venom enters a body, it is circulated by the lymphatic system, as well as the circulatory system.

mammal: a warm-blooded animal with a backbone that has hair or fur and, if female, produces milk for its young.

marsupial: a type of mammal with a pouch in which the young develop after they are born.

medusa: one of the two forms of cnidarians, especially the adult form of a jellyfish—free-swimming, rounded, and with a mouth that points downward.

mellitin: the main ingredient in bee venom responsible for the pain of a sting. It is also a strong anti-inflammatory agent.

mesosoma: the main or middle part of an arachnid's or an insect's body.

Glossary

metasoma: the last section of an arachnid's or an insect's body.

mimicry: an adaptation by which a species looks or sounds like another species in order to fool predators or prey. *Batesian mimicry:* a species appears to possess the same traits as the creature it is mimicking, but does not actually have those traits. *Mullerian mimicry:* a species possesses the same traits of the species it is imitating.

mollusk: a soft-bodied, typically shell-making animal with a muscular foot for movement.

monotreme: an egg-laying mammal. Platypuses and echnidas are the only monotremes on earth.

myotoxin: a toxin that affects the skeletal muscles, causing paralysis and preventing the victim from breathing.

necrotoxin: a toxin that kills tissue cells.

nematocysts: stinging cells on the tentacles of jellyfish and other cnidarians.

nemertine: a type of long, aquatic worm, also called a *ribbon worm* or a *proboscis worm* because of its long feeding tube.

neurotoxin: a toxin that causes damage to nerve cells, often resulting in paralysis.

nocturnal: active at night.

nudibranch: a type of shell-less mollusk, also called a *sea slug*.

ophidiphobia: fear of snakes.

opisthoglyph: a rear-fanged snake.

ovipositor: an insect's egg-laying tube. In bees, wasps, and ants, it has modified into a stinger.

papain: an enzyme that breaks down the toxins in bee and other venom. It is from the papaya fruit and found in meat tenderizers.

parasite: an animal or plant that receives something, generally food, from another animal or plant and gives nothing in return. Parasites may harm or even kill their hosts. Verb form: *parasitize*.

parotid glands: saliva-producing glands. In toads, this pair of glands, located behind their eyes, secretes sticky, white poison for self-defense.

pedicellariae: small pincers on stalks used for cleaning and self-defense found on echinoderms, especially sea urchins.

pedipalps: the pair of body parts near an arachnid's mouth shaped like short legs and used to sense and handle food.

pelagic: living on the open sea.

photic zone: the upper area of oceans and other large bodies of water where sunlight can reach.

pincers: claw-like body parts of insects, scorpions, and other animals used for grasping.

planula: the larva of a jellyfish or other cnidarian that attaches to a base and becomes a polyp.

poison: in biology, a toxic substance that harms a victim when it is eaten or absorbed through the skin; *poisonous* animals, which include toads, salamanders, some birds and frogs, sea cucumbers, a variety of insects and other animals, have toxins in their skin, organs, or other body parts, and some can ooze these toxins.

polychaete: a type of aquatic worm generally covered with bristles. Also called *bristle worm*.

polyp: one of the two forms of cnidarians—tube-like, fixed to a base, and with a mouth that points upwards, such as a sea anemone or coral.

poriferan: a member of the sponge family. Sponges are aquatic, immobile, animals that pump water through their bodies to filter out food particles.

prehensors: the pair of specialized poison claws located beneath a centipede's head.

prevenom: a type of venom produced by scorpions that is less deadly, but more rapid and painful to predators and prey.

primate: a mammal with five nailed fingers, opposable thumbs (able to touch the other fingers), three kinds of teeth, and a well-developed brain.

proboscis: the feeding-tube of many insects, worms, and mollusks.

procoagulant: an agent that causes blood clots to form.

protein: an organic compound made of amino acids that carries out important body functions.

proteroglyph: a snake with fixed front fangs.

radial symmetry: the balanced distribution of duplicate body parts around a central point, with no left or right sides.

radula: the toothed "tongue" of some mollusks.

reef: an aquatic structure made up of hard mineral deposits. A *coral reef* is comprised of the stony cases of living and dead corals.

reflex-bleeding: a defense used by some insects in which they ooze blood and bad-tasting toxins from their leg joints.

reptile: a cold-blooded animal with a backbone and dry, scaly skin, which may lay eggs or bear live young. Reptiles include snakes, lizards, alligators, crocodiles, and turtles.

rostrum: in insects and arachnids, a type of "beak," used for piercing and sucking up plant or animal food.

self-anointing: the practice by hedgehogs and other animals of applying a strong-smelling substance to fur or spines, possibly in self-defense, to attract a mate and/or to get rid of parasites.

setae: stiff hairs or bristles.

siphon: a tube-like organ found in aquatic insects and other animals that acts as a snorkel to take in oxygen.

solenoglyph: a snake with front fangs that fold. Also called a *viper*.

stylet: in worms and insects, a thin sharp tube for injecting and drawing up venom and liquefied food.

symbiosis: two dissimilar beings living together in a mutually beneficial relationship.

systemic reaction: a bad response to toxins, allergens, or other substances that involves the whole body.

telson: the final section of the metasoma of an arachnid's or insect's body, e.g. the last part of a scorpion's tail-like abdomen.

tentacles: long, flexible organs used for feeding, feeling, grasping, and, in cnidarians, stinging.

terrestrial: living on land.

tetrodotoxin: a potent neurotoxin produced by puffer fish, some species of octopus, and other animals.

toxin: technically, a poisonous substance made up mostly of protein produced by a plant or animal (see *biotoxin*), but also used to mean any harmful substance that causes ill health. See *batrachotoxin, cantharidin, cardiotoxin, conotoxin, hemotoxin, holothurin, lucibufagins, myotoxin, necrotoxin, neurotoxin, tetrodotoxin*.

urticate: to sting or itch. Some insects and arachnids have *urticating* hairs or spines that shed or break off easily to irritate predators.

venom: biotoxins injected by a wide variety of animals for hunting, self-defense, or protection of offspring. *Venomous* animals, which include snakes, spiders, bees, a number of fish species, and other animals, use fangs, stingers, spines, and other devices to inject these toxins.

Index